BRITISH RAILWAYS ILLUSTRATED

ANNUAL
Number 12

IRWELL PRESS

ILLUSTRATED

ated Annual No.12

Now We Are Twelve!

Welcome to British Railways Illustrated Annual No.12. All New Photographs and Articles!

You'll Remember those Black and White Days

BRITISH **RAILWAYS** ILLUSTRATED
Vol. 12 No.6 March 2003

IRWELL PRESS at the ALLY PALLY SHOW - 22 & 23 March

ANOTHER VISIT TO SHEFFIELD VICTORIA
ELECTRIC BLUES · LATE DAY FREIGHTS · OVER THE TOP
ISLAND INTERLUDE · TWO SOUTH WALES SHEDS · PADDINGTON 1961
A EUSTON PILOT · THEY USED TO SET ON FIRE! · FOURUM

Pick up a copy of the
monthly magazine
BRITISH RAILWAYS ILLUSTRATED
at a newsagent, specialist book
and model shop or direct from
the publisher every month.
Only £3.30

CONTENTS

EDITORIAL MATTERS
Contributions,
submissions, photographs or whatever
(remember the contributor must
address and attend to
copyright and insurance on goods sent),
readers' letters, bouquets
and brickbats for
British Railways Illustrated
must be addressed to Editor,
Chris Hawkins
at 59A, High Street, Clophill,
Bedfordshire MK45 4BE
E-mail chris@irwellpress.co.uk
Tel.01525 861888 or
Fax. 01525 862044
Printed & Bound by
Newton Printing, London
Copyright :- Irwell Press Ltd. 2003

Cover photograph. Meeting at
Teignmouth in June 1959, with 2-8-0
3813 and new Warship D804
AVENGER. Stanley Creer, The
Transport Treasury.

Rear cover. A1 Pacific (for more see
inside) 60149 AMADIS resting at
Kings Cross, 2 June 1962. Frank
Hornby.

Frontispiece. Classic George, with
44943 at one of his favourite
locations, Westerleigh North
Junction. Look out for more of his
work in *British Railways Illustrated*
soon. George Heiron, The Transport
Treasury.

IRWELL PRESS
No.1 in Railway Publishing

UPWEY AWAYDAY, 19 July 1958
D.W. Winkworth

34099 LYNMOUTH passing Parkstone with 9.45am Pines Express from Bournemouth West. Note lamp headcode for passenger train peculiar to Somerset & Dorset section. Photograph D.W. Winkworth.

An annual engagement the writer enjoyed for several years was a weekend visit to friends living in the Bournemouth area during which there would be a Saturday visit to a railway location to record, by note and camera, the passing traffic. The *modus operandi* was for visitor and host's son to work their way to the chosen point in a series of hops while the host, hostess and daughter complete with viands for a picnic would follow by car.

For 19 July 1958 the venue was a point south of Upwey, between Dorchester and Weymouth. A grassed bridge over the railway was selected as the parking point which would inconvenience farming requirements as little as possible. The advance party set off on the 8.46am from Pokesdown (5.40am from Waterloo to Weymouth) hauled by 34018 AXMINSTER. At Bournemouth the 9.13am train (8.48am New Milton to Swansea High Street) was in the charge of 2-6-0 76069 and this was taken as far as Parkstone where a break was made to see Somerset & Dorset traffic from Bournemouth West station passing northwards. Class 5 Standard 4-6-0 73087 was working

UP TRAINS 19 JULY 1958	
12.20pm to Waterloo	34041 WILTON
12.40pm to Bristol (Temple Meads)	5015 KINGSWEAR CASTLE
12.50pm to Yeovil (Pen Mill)	1453
1.20pm to Waterloo	34018 AXMINSTER (a)
1.35pm to Cardiff (General)	6352
1.45pm to Bristol (Temple Meads)	6399 (b)
1.55pm to Swindon	5990 DORFORD HALL (c)
2.5pm to Maiden Newton	4133
2.20pm to Eastleigh	30784 SIR NEROVENS
2.30pm to Westbury	5983 HENLEY HALL
3.15pm Empty coaches	
to Hamworthy Junction	35014 NEDERLAND HALL (c)
3.15pm Light engine	
to Bournemouth Central Loco	30482
3.30pm to Maiden Newton	7782
3.50pm to Waterloo	30535 + 30774 SIR GAHERIS
3.40pm to Paddington	5093 UPTON CASTLE (b)
4.10pm to Paddington	5981 FRENSHAM HALL
4.5pm to Birmingham (SH)	5942 DOLDOWLOD HALL (c)
4.40pm to Bournemouth Central	30765 SIR GARETH
LE	4562
5.0pm Freight	
to Bournemouth Central Goods	30864 SIR MARTIN FROBISHER (d)
5.35pm to Waterloo	34006 BUDE + 34043 COMBE MARTIN
5.41pm to Bournemouth Central	31620

(a) Banked by 34043
(b) Banked by 4166
(c) Banked by 5978 BODINNICK HALL
(d) Banked by 0-6-0PT
LE Light Engine

DOWN TRAINS 19 JULY 1958	
8.30am ex-Paddington	5093 UPTON CASTLE
9.10am ex-Bristol (Temple Meads)	5981 FRENSHAM HALL
8.30am ex-Waterloo	34043 COMBE MARTIN
12.15pm ex-Dorchester South	31620
12.10pm ex-Yeovil (Pen Mill)	4133
9.24am ex-Waterloo	35014 NEDERLAND LINE
11.43am ex-Westbury	4962 RAGLEY HALL
9.27am ex-Wimbledon	30774 SIR GAHERIS
12.30pm ex-Westbury	5975 WINSLOW HALL
10.30am ex-Waterloo	34006 BUDE
1.55pm LE ex-Dorchester South	30535
1.35pm ex-Yeovil (Pen Mill)	7782
1.10pm ex-Bournemouth Central	30482
11.22am ex-Waterloo	30765 SIR GARETH
2.55pm ex-Maiden Newton	4133
Unidentified passenger	33007
12.45pm ex-Bristol (Temple Meads)	5919 WORSLEY HALL
LE	4562
12.35pm ex-Waterloo	30902 WELLINGTON
12.30pm ex-Paddington	7917 NORTH ASTON HALL
3.16pm ex-Bournemouth Central	30310
4.30pm ex-Maiden Newton	7782
11.5am ex-Wolverhampton (LL)	5964 WOLSELEY HALL

the 9.25am Manchester and Liverpool service followed by 34099 LYNMOUTH on the Pines Express, 73047 on the 9.55am Leeds and 44888 on the 10.5am to Derby.

One of the curiosities in this part of the country was the headcode used on the front of the locomotives. For the Southern Region white discs or, at night, lamps denoted the route the train was using; for the route from Bournemouth Central to Weymouth one disc above each buffer was used

chimney and another over the right-hand buffer (viewed from the front); goods trains had a lamp in front of the chimney and another over the left-hand buffer while light engines just carried a lamp in front of the chimney. The Western Region used the standard BR code describing the class of train being worked with lamps rather than discs.

Having spent about an hour at Parkstone the 10.21am train was then boarded. This was the 8.37am service from Eastleigh hauled by

for passenger trains. For through trains from Waterloo the code had to be changed at Bournemouth Central. The Somerset & Dorset code was to indicate the type of train rather than the route although on SR metals it served a dual purpose. The passenger trains carried a lamp (rather than discs) in front of the

30784 SIR NEROVENS. Arrival at Upwey was in advance of the support vehicle with the picnic so the 12.24pm from there (12.15pm from Dorchester South) was sampled because it had the attraction of terminating at Melcombe Regis station at Weymouth rather than the Town station. The engine was U class 2-6-0 31620. Return to Upwey was on the 12.50pm train from the main station, powered by GW 0-4-2T 1453.

Upwey was situated on the climb out of Weymouth up to the summit at Bincombe tunnel. The gradient stiffened from 1 in 74 to the 1 in 50 at Upwey then eased slightly to 1 in 52 at Upwey Wishing Well halt before the top of the incline at the tunnel. Assistance was required for trains of any magnitude and this was usually provided by a banking engine not coupled to the train. This banker would halt at the signal box by the tunnel then go into the siding between the running lines to await a suitable opportunity to return the four miles to Weymouth. The alternative was to double-head trains through to Dorchester where the assisting engine would be uncoupled. This usually involved Southern Region trains to Dorchester South. Apart from the awkward layout there which necessitated a reversal to get into the up platform there was the drawback of different braking

5093 UPTON CASTLE passing Upwey & Broadway with the 8.30am from Paddington boat train. 2-6-2 tank 4166 on banking duty in the siding awaits the next call. Photograph D.W. Winkworth.

34041 WILTON pauses at Upwey & Broadwey on Bournemouth duty 410 with the 12.20pm Weymouth to Waterloo service. Photograph D.W. Winkworth.

pressures when a WR engine was assisting.

The gradient provided extra interest for the enthusiast in that the up trains would perhaps have a banking engine or be double-headed and exhaust effects would be enhanced. Conversely the down trains nipped by Upwey with the minimum of effort. Upwey had been the junction for the Abbotsbury branch but by this date that had closed and Upwey Junction, as the station had been known, became Upwey and Broadwey. In tabulating. the passing traffic the return passages of the banking engines running light have been ignored. There are no great surprises insofar as the down traffic was concerned although the appearance of Schools class WELLINGTON on the 12.35pm from Waterloo was pleasing, as was the passing of T9 4-4-0 30310.

2-6-2T 4133 runs through Upwey down to Melcombe Regis with the 12.10pm train from Yeovil (Pen Mill). (Obervers' support vehicle is parked by the right-hand side of the bridge). Photograph D.W. Winkworth.

You'll Remember those Black and White Days...

Nine Elms duty 45 was for a Merchant Navy Pacific to work the 9.24am from Waterloo to Weymouth so there was no surprise when 35014 NEDERLAND LINE swept past Upwey with the train. Photograph D.W. Winkworth.

However, the train hauled by Q1 0-6-0 33007 could not be reconciled with the timetable. Its train consisted of London Midland Region coaches suggesting that it might have come off the Somerset & Dorset as a special.

Northwards out of Weymouth the 5.0pm freight to Bournemouth Central Goods produced 30864 SIR MARTIN FROBISHER. It was not a fluke working but all to plan, being part of Bournemouth shed's duty 400. Also double-heading by light Pacifics of the 5.35pm from Weymouth was a booked working. H15 4-6-0 30482 was supposed to have banked the 3.15pm empty coaching stock but instead Hall 5978 did the job, leaving 30482 to run light to Bournemouth.

Western Region 63XX class 2-6-0 6352 attacks the climb to Bincombe tunnel with the 1.35pm Weymouth to Cardiff (General) train. Photograph D.W. Winkworth.

You'll Remember those Black and White Days...

30784 SIR NEROVENS does not need assistance with the six coach 2.20pm Weymouth to Eastleigh train as it approaches Upwey & Broadwey. The leading 3-set 426 is one of two dozen allocated to local services and consists of BSKs (second brake corridors) 3746 and 3747 and CK (composite corridor) 5649 giving a total of 144 seats of which 24 were first class. The other, unidentified, 3-set is of LSWR origin. Photograph D.W. Winkworth.

The half-day's haul was not a bad catch. A total of 33 different engines of which there were representatives from 17 classes was the score and this excepts sightings en route. For sheer quantity the WR Halls with ten head the list; after that came four SR light Pacifics, three King Arthurs and two WR 63XX 2-6-0s. All the rest were 'singles'. The family left the visitor to wend his way back which involved U class 31620 to Bournemouth Central and then the 7.50pm thence to Pokesdown with 34006 BUDE at the front. Would that it could be repeated now!

Below. Pannier tank 7782 working the 3.30pm Weymouth to Maiden Newton local train near Upwey. Photograph D.W. Winkworth.

Class H15 4-6-0 30482 trundles down to Melcombe Regis with the 1.10pm local service from Eastleigh on duty 73.

Q class 0-6-0 30535 halted by signal at Upwey while running light (1.55pm ex-Dorchester South) to Weymouth shed. Photograph D.W. Winkworth.

You'll Remember those Black and White Days...

5093 UPTON CASTLE returning to Paddington with the up 3.40pm Channel Islands boat train with 4166 giving assistance in the rear. The train identification number 387 has been chalked on the smokebox door. On the Southern Region such numbers were not used west of Bournemouth. Photograph D.W. Winkworth.

5942 DOLDOWLOD HALL tackling the 1 in 74 gradient with the 4.5pm Weymouth to Birmingham (Snow Hill) with 5978 BODINNICK HALL assisting in the rear. Photograph D.W. Winkworth.

A shining ensemble: 7917 NORTH ASTON HALL shuts off steam while passing Upwey with the 12.30pm from Paddington. Photograph D.W. Winkworth.

Veteran T9 4-4-0 30310 drifts by Upwey with the 3.16pm all stations from Bournemouth Central train. Photograph D.W. Winkworth.

From Distant to Distant
Ais Gill Summit, 2 July 1953
Notes by Bryan Wilson

This remarkable sequence comprehensively illustrates Ais Gill, from Distant to Distant, in July 1953 when 'modernisation' meant little more than the appearance of a few BR Standard locomotives, and even they were not much in evidence up here. The first Ais Gill signal box opened with a single line in August 1875, with the Block Telegraph from the start. The line from Hawes Junction ('Garsdale' from 1932) to Mallerstang, the next box beyond Ais Gill to the north, was doubled from 4 October 1875 and both passenger and goods services commenced on 1 May the following year. The line reaches 1,151 feet above sea level in Blea Moor tunnel, 1,145ft at Dent station and peaks at 1,169 at Ais Gill before falling steeply to sea level at Carlisle. Indeed, nearly twelve of the forty-seven miles from Petteril Bridge Junction are at 1 in 100, gruelling stuff in the Up direction with a less than perfect engine on a wild night. Having set the scene, let us survey this summit from south to north, from one Distant signal to the next. We are atop the Down Home signal, which is on the Up side, as we shall see later. The points immediately ahead of us lead from the Up Refuge Siding with the back of No.11 Disc in view. Ahead is the Up Starter (No.3). The culvert beneath the line boasts quite ornate stonework from the 'no accountant watching' days of fond memory.

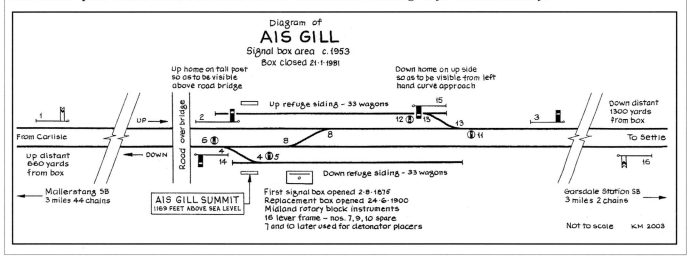

Diagram of
AIS GILL
Signal box area c.1953
Box closed 21·1·1981

Up home on tall post so as to be visible above road bridge

Down home on up side so as to be visible from left hand curve approach

Up refuge siding - 33 wagons

Down distant 1300 yards from box

From Carlisle

To Settle

Up distant 660 yards from box

Down refuge siding - 33 wagons

AIS GILL SUMMIT
1169 FEET ABOVE SEA LEVEL

Mallerstang SB
3 miles 44 chains

First signal box opened 2·8·1875
Replacement box opened 24·6·1900
Midland rotary block instruments
16 lever frame – nos. 7,9,10 spare
7 and 10 later used for detonator placers

Garsdale Station SB
3 miles 2 chains

Not to scale   KM 2003

You'll Remember those Black and White Days...

Ais Gill Up Starting signal (No.3). A standard LMS tubular post upper quadrant signal. The diamond cut out indicates a Track Circuit and its centre is 12ft above rail level; the post is shaded behind to make it conspicuous. It is 1ft 10ins from the centre of the green spectacle to the top of the post. What's more, the ladder is at an incline of 1 in 12. These were the Signal Engineer's stipulations so no excuses now for modellers not to get them right!

This is the signal that the photographer climbed for the first picture, a classic Midland lower quadrant (Lever 15). It's the Down Home, a tapered wooden post and wooden arm. The post has a black patch to highlight the diamond. Three stay wires are necessary at this altitude to keep it stable. An antique revolving disc signal (No.12) guards the exit from the Up Refuge.

'Crab' 2-6-0 42868 of Agecroft shed and a rare beast hereabouts, passes the box (behind the train) with a Brindle Heath (Manchester) to Carlisle Class 'E' freight. That Midland lower quadrant is well sighted for the curve of the approaching train.

Looking north to the looming Wild Boar Fell. No.11 Disc is facing us, positioned in the 'six foot' between the main lines and the Midland Down Home is prominent. The old outlet disc is painted white at back and side so that no one falls over it in the dark. Overbridge 132 is ahead; it carries a track to Hellgill, as well as being the county boundary between Westmorland and Yorkshire.

Looking south from the top of the Up Home signal. The complete trackwork controlled by Ais Gill box can be seen, also the ground signals to and from the Down Refuge Siding (levers 5 and 6). Also visible are the Summit Boards either side of the tracks and the 259¾ MP.

The box in its setting. Real Midland splendour as Wild Boar Fell broods over us from the north. The houses (the only habitation in sight) are the Company's Aisgill Moor cottages for employees. The tin shack, coal storage bin and platelayers' hut with its lazy smoke ooze atmosphere. But it is the 2nd of July you say. Remember, this is Ais Gill, where summer comes late and leaves early!

The first box here opened with the line in August 1875. This one dates from 24 June 1900 and is of Midland 'Type 2B' with 5ft 1in deep windows in front and 3ft 6in deep at the ends. The '2B' design lasted from 1892 to 1901. The tubular steel staircase is a modern replacement and it is certainly true that Midland stairs had a propensity to rot. The fire buckets are 'BR'. And what does that amazing outfall pipe do? Note the telegraph wires crossing from down side to up at the box...

Black 5 45056 of Sheffield makes it to the top with an Up Class 'H'. There are 'fitted' vehicles up front but the train is probably too heavy to run at 'E' speed. There are a few leaks but the engine is in good exterior condition. A railwayman stands with a farmer adjacent to the stone wall waiting for the noise of the passing train to cease, when conversation will resume.

You'll Remember those Black and White Days...

A good view of the revolving disc signal applying to movements from the Down Refuge (No.5). Note the ground around the Summit sign has been carefully tended, as has the ballast. No weeds, no rubbish, just 'pride in the job'. The Down Starting signal ahead (No.14) has the diamond high up, again for sighting purposes.

Overbridge No.132 with the number painted on one side and cast plate on the other. The commencement of 1 in 100 down can be seen ahead, and look where the Up Home has had to be put to give adequate sighting to climbing trains. The diamond, too, is high. The Up Distant can be seen just beyond where the lines fall away.

This is an exception in the series; this is the mid-1960s and Class 5 44671 (always a Kingmoor locomotive) climbs the last half mile to the Summit with an up class 'F'. Over to the right here the waters of the Eden and the Ure commence, the former ending in the Solway Firth and the other in the North Sea.

Ais Gill Up Distant, a standard LMS signal on a tubular post, painted according to the '1939 specification' (almost) which required black up to 1ft above the balance lever casting, then alternate black and white strips approximately 2ft wide to the post top. Tubular post distant signals were considered to be important markers, hence the prominent colouring. Again, one for the modellers. Note also the wire along the bank on the opposite, Down side, high enough to keep out of the snow and falling sharply as it gets to the signal.

The photographer is standing by the Up Distant – with permission we hope. The signal wire can be seen descending to the right of the buffer beam of Black 5 44943 of Leeds – in the days when Holbeck was 20A. The train is a Class 'H' with a load of pipes and things military. Being unbraked, these will take some holding on the way down to Carlisle. The loco was new to Holbeck in December 1945 and stayed nearly eighteen years.

Ais Gill viaduct (Bridge 137 to the Engineer) at 260m 54ch from St Pancras, four stone spans and 87 yards long. The arches were all equal at 45 feet and the structure was 75ft above the real 'Ais Ghyll'. The ridge beyond is Mallerstang Edge, which gave its name to the next signal box to the north, 'Mallerstang'.

You'll Remember those Black and White Days...

Another Kingmoor Class 5, 44725, crosses Ais Gill viaduct with a three coach Up local passenger of crimson and cream coaches. The elaborate bridge beyond carries only a farm track.

A better view of that bridge as Black 5 45088 of Leicester climbs up to Ais Gill with a Class 'E' freight. Not a leak anywhere and the fireman in his seat – she must be in good shape.

Royal Scots came to the line in August 1943 after bridge rebuilding to enable them to do so was complete south of Skipton. 46103 ROYAL SCOTS FUSILIER is north of Ais Gill with a Down express. The crew should have an easy time now, as it is predominantly downhill all the way to Carlisle.

The post that says what the Settle & Carlisle, and particularly Ais Gill, was all about –hard work.

You'll Remember those Black and White Days...

ALFRED THE GREAT AT BOURNEMOUTH WEST

D.W. Winkworth

ALFRED THE GREAT was one of a trio of Britannia Standard Class 7 4-6-2s allocated to the Southern Region to power the designated 1951 Festival train, the Royal Wessex. In the event, it appears to have had no more than one round trip with the train from London Waterloo to Weymouth, the Southern authorities choosing to employ it on the Bournemouth Belle instead. Of the three engines, 70004 WILLIAM SHAKESPEARE was incarcerated in the Festival of Britain exhibition site on the south bank of the Thames and was not released until the close of the exhibition. Meanwhile, 70014 IRON DUKE at first ran from Nine Elms and then went to Stewarts Lane shed to work the Golden Arrow service, leaving 70009 to operate out of Nine Elms shed. The accompanying photographs of 70009 iIlcude bowler and trilby hatted staff in attendance at Bournemouth West suggesting this was shortly after the engine had arrived on the SR in late May 1951

and was under close observation. Indeed these pictures could have been taken on 6 June when the locomotive made its first round trip on the Belle, such is its pristine condition.

At this time the train left Waterloo at 12.30pm, called at Southampton Central at 1.58pm and arrived at Bournemouth Central at 2.40pm going on to Bournemouth West where the down trip was concluded at 2.52pm. The return timing was 4.34pm from Bournemouth West, 4.45pm from Bournemouth Central and 5.20pm from Southampton Central with an arrival at Waterloo at 6.50pm.

For the first year of operation in 1931, when it left Waterloo at 10.30am, a portion of this all-Pullman train went on to serve Poole (compulsory call), Wareham (non-Pullman connection to Swanage), Dorchester and Weymouth with arrival there at 1.45pm, the rest of the train terminating at Bournemouth West. This

(Weymouth) was a destination too far insofar as day excursion traffic was concerned and it disappeared from the timetable after its first and only summer. Thereafter there was a lot of experimentation with timings, in particular the up service which, at various times, got back to Waterloo at 6.45pm, 6.55pm, 7.18pm, 8.30pm, 8.45pm and 9.40pm.

To return to 1951 and 70009's advent on the Southern, it was a nice out-and-home job for the Nine Elms enginemen who booked on to the shed at 11.20am with the engine already prepared for them. They were booked off Nine Elms at 11.35am and into Waterloo at 11.56am where they backed the engine on to its train. Departure was at 12.30pm and arrival at Bournemouth West at 2.52pm, following which the empty train was propelled into the carriage sidings and the engine released to work around the triangle at Branksome and then into Branksome shed. After about an hour it was

time to leave the shed and couple up to the empty stock and propel into the West station ready for the 4.34pm departure. Traffic at this terminus, so far as the Belle was concerned, was never very heavy and if an unhurried departure was valued by passengers then this was the place to join. It saved frantic rushing around at the Central station trying to locate your coach and seat allocation.

The train was booked into Waterloo at 6.50pm with the crew to be relieved at the buffer stops by another Nine Elms pair who would work the engine light back to the shed. Human nature being what it is the engine duties clerk knew the carrot of booking off to go home immediately on arrival was conducive to punctual running and an incentive for the fireman who might possibly have had hopes of an assignation with his 'bird' for the evening. The older man would have seen all that in his time and would doubtless co-operate. Whether on this occasion it was to work like that remained to be seen, even as the fireman worked the coal forward in the tender in readiness. The drawback was that drivers tended, when an inspector was on the footplate, to run closely to schedule without indulging in 'fireworks'. Anyhow the fireman might well be faced with receiving 'suitable advice' (as the term went) from the inspector as to the desirability of emitting steam from the safety valves in station precincts.

It remains to mention the stock – what can be seen of it. CAR No.27 was a Third Brake Parlour car, with

You'll Remember those Black and White Days...

8-wheeled bogies, seating 30 passengers and weighing 40 tons. There would be another of the same type at the other end of the train. The Appendix to the Carriage Working Notice set out the summer and winter compositions of the train which would embrace about 10 to 12 vehicles of various types (First Parlour, First Kitchen, Third Parlour, Third Kitchen and Third Brake Parlour) of which about ten would be required for any one trip with additions at times of heavy traffic such as weekends.

Diesel Dawn
Newton Abbot

The first diesel hydraulics had come to Newton Abbot in the late 1950s and it saw the sort of lavish provision which characterised dieselisation on the WR until the money began to get tighter about 1964. The old locomotive works was converted into a Maintenance Shop, which involved the installation of a completely new traverser at 90 degrees to the old one. Fit for a Doncaster or a Crewe (or even a Swindon) it gave access to just four roads. Here it is more or less complete about 1961, with new Warships D826 JUPITER and D836 POWERFUL. Traffic changes and the end of the diesel hydraulics brought about the demise of '83A' in the early 1970s.

You'll Remember those Black and White Days...

Mike King, a leading light in the three-volume 'Illustrated History of Southern Wagons' from OPC/Ian Allan and a must for wagon enthusiasts (the books that is, not Mike) describes four wagons from the Charles Roberts collection, distributed by Terry Walsh and available from Roger Carpenter. The Charles Roberts Works were at Horbury Junction, adjacent to the L&Y Wakefield-Barnsley line in the West Riding of Yorkshire. Ordered on 28 September 1931, this RCH 1923 specification 12 ton 8-plank mineral wagon was completed in October and registered with the Southern Railway that same month as No.576. The number is just visible on the registration plate at the left-hand end of the solebar. It is in Charles Roberts yard before dispatch to its owner. Livery is black with plain white lettering – one of the most common and certainly the most economical for the purchaser. Despite being No.10, it could well have been Mr Patience's only wagon.

Ordered the same day was Challis wagon No.20, almost identical to No.10 – the two firms were perhaps connected in some way, such is the similarity. This wagon was SR registration 577, again just visible on the plate. All main line railway companies maintained a register of private-owner wagons, to ensure that they conformed to Railway Clearing House (RCH) specifications and were maintained by their owners in a fit state. With less industry, the SR registered total was small – a mere 1,600 vehicles (including various tanks) between 1923 and about 1960.

A very different type of private-owner wagon, 8 ton all-steel flat No.105, painted grey (what other colour did the Admiralty use?) with black underframe and fittings. It was probably built before 1914. There is no registration plate, indicating that the wagon was to be used only within the extensive Dockyard railway and would not normally travel on the main lines. The Dockyard had a large fleet of internal-user wagons, including opens, covered goods wagons, tanks and various flat wagons such as this, used for moving bulky items of equipment around the complex.

Charles Roberts also built and repaired railway company wagons. This is ex-LBSCR ballast hopper No.10517 as reconstructed in 1930 and repainted in Engineer's Department red oxide livery as SR No.62799. All thirty wagons, to SR diagram 1755, were sent to Roberts at about this time for the hopper bottom mechanism to be rebuilt so that it discharged within the 'four-foot' instead of the previous arrangement whereby it discharged alongside the track. Note the canvas covers to the axleboxes and springs – designed to keep the stone dust away from the moving parts.

Big 'Uns... and Others

That uniquely impressive front end, in this instance 46227 DUCHESS OF DEVONSHIRE, a Polmadie engine, at home, on 19 June 1960. The 'others' on this occasion are a motley collection of the 'lesser breeds'; most curiously one of the new Swindon Inter-City sets and, more conventionally, 0-4-4T 55169, a Black Five behind and, beyond, one of Polmadie's little Standard 3MT 2-6-0s, 77009. Photograph Frank Hornby.

46234 DUCHESS OF ABERCORN at Willesden, about 1962, in varied company – 2-6-4T 42586 in front and an original Patriot in line behind. Photograph Frank Hornby.

Crewe North was the true home of 'the big 'uns' (it was where the name was coined after all, and was probably only used there) so it's no surprise that home-grown 46228 DUCHESS OF RUTLAND should make such a fine sight, putting the otherwise magnificent Jubilee 45606 FALKLAND ISLANDS completely in the shade. Photograph Frank Hornby.

It's definitely 'beauty and the beast' now as a DMU clatters into Birmingham New Street on 3 April 1960. It's a shame the diesel set will obscure the eye and ear boggling sight of 46233 DUCHESS OF SUTHERLAND, though those lads down by the track at the front won't be bothered. Can this be even imagined today? Photograph Stanley Creer, The Transport Treasury.

You'll Remember those Black and White Days...

FREEMAN'S FORAYS
Kings Cross to York and Return
Saturday 15th July 1961

Leslie Freeman made many railway trips in the 1950s and 1960s, searching out steam and rejecting diesels, recording his experiences and impressions along the way. A number of these Freeman's Forays *are being published in* British Railways Illustrated *magazine. Keep a look out for them!*

Above. Leslie Freeman breaks the journey at Grantham, where the engine changing, shunting and all the activity associated with the adjacent shed could be contemplated. 60148 ABOYEUR, which had conveyed our intrepid reporter from Kings Cross, departs northward with 'The West Riding', the 8am Kings Cross-Leeds. Photograph L.R. Freeman, The Transport Treasury.

For some while before this trip, I had been considering going on a purely 'copping' journey to the north wanting, in particular, to see some North Eastern engines before they were all scrapped. I finally settled on York and decided that I would do it at once before dieselisation proceeded any further. An additional reason for choosing the East Coast route was to travel with, and photograph, some Gresley Pacifics, particularly A3s. In order to add some interest, I also decided to break my journey for an hour or so at Grantham. So, in high hopes, I made my way to Kings Cross on this fine Saturday morning for my first real excursion on the East Coast main line.

For the journey to Grantham I decided to catch 'The West Riding', the 8am to Leeds and Bradford. I hoped, of course, for an A3 but I found its twelve corridors headed by an A1, 60148 ABOYEUR. We left 40 seconds late, slipped as we went into Gas Works Tunnel and climbed fairly slowly up to Finsbury Park, after which 60148 was really set to work as shown in the log above.

Miles		Min	Secs	Speed
0.0	Kings Cross	0	00	
	Holloway S. Box Up	5	00	
2.5	Finsbury Park	7	20	
5.0	Wood Green	10	18	51mph
9.2	New Barnet	14	57	54mph
12.7	Potters Bar	18	40	56.5mph
17.7	Hatfield	23	35	61mph
20.3	Welwyn Garden City	25	43	73mph
	Easing at Welwyn Viaduct			66mph
25.0	Knebworth	29	56	68.5mph
28.6	Stevenage	33	05	
31.9	Hitchin (arrival after slow approach)	37	20	

We were thus four minutes early after this good start, on which I only noted two engines, V2 60845 at Kings Cross and B1 61364 coming off Top Shed. There were three more locomotives at Hitchin, WDs 90151 and 90665 in the yard and on an up ballast train respectively, and 3F 43766 in the Midland yard. We waited the 4 minutes, all but 10 seconds, then 60148 set off without a slip to Grantham - *See table p31.*

So ended what up to Yaxley had been a fine effort. Unfortunately not quite

enough was made up Stoke and our arrival was just one minute late. Still, it would be a pedant who would complain about that! Apart from the locomotives seen en route, I noted that the closed stations north of Hitchin were either recently demolished, like Three Counties, Offord and Abbots Ripton, or in course of demolition like Essendine, where the down platform had gone. The other stations on Stoke bank had also gone. Other observations included WD 90730 at Biggleswade, 9F 92181 on an up goods near

Miles		Min	Secs	Speed
0.0	Hitchin	0	00	
5.1	Arlesey	6	35	
9.2	Biggleswade	9	58	73mph
12.2	Sandy	12	20	76mph
	Tempsford			80mph
19.8	St Neots	17	56	71mph
	Offord			70mph
27.0	Huntingdon North	23	58	72mph
31.6	Abbots Ripton	28	06	66.5mph
35.5	Connington South	31	10	76mph
44.5	Peterborough North	44	58	(pws Yaxley/slow to P'boro)
47.6	Werrington Junction	48	28	(signals after Tallington)
56.7	Essendine	57	50	55/56mph
60.3	Little Bytham	61	50	54mph
65.2	Corby Glen	67	20	53mph (MP99)
68.2	Stoke	70	45	52.5mph
73.6	Grantham	77	10	

Tempsford and, at Huntingdon, a demolition train in the East station where the westbound island platform was in course of demolition. At Holme, the station was gone but the Ramsey branch still remained. There were two more WDs at Yaxley, 90130 and 91058, the former on an up coal train, along with A3 60111 ENTERPRISE on an up express. At Peterborough there was a V2, 60853, a B1 61328 and a 9F 92201; two N2 0-6-2Ts, 69549 and 69580, were on carriage pilot duties. Essendine had a K3 2-6-0, 61860, in the yard.

I alighted at Grantham and then spent over an hour and a half observing; a very interesting time it was with not very many diesels about and, at times, a queue of trains on the up line. On shed or shunting around the station were Pacifics 60076 GALOPIN, 60105 VICTOR WILD, 60121 SILURIAN and 60146 PEREGRINE, V2 60905 and L1 2-6-4Ts 67751, 67752, 67773, 67774, 67776 and 67791 – of these 67752, 67774 and 67776 were acting as pilots. Now for train observations.

10.11   A4 60008 DWIGHT D EISENHOWER, up fast, 8.10 Leeds-Kings Cross; A3 60077 THE WHITE KNIGHT, off shed.

10.24   A1 60117 BOIS ROUSSEL, up fast, 'The West Riding' 8.21 Leeds-Kings Cross.

10.26   L1 67756 arrived with 9.40 ex-Nottingham Victoria (two minutes early); O2s 63982 and 63963 arrived light from the north and went on shed.

10.38   A4 60032 GANNET, down fast, 8.52 Kings Cross-Leeds; A3 60049 GALTEE MORE and V2 60905 off shed to take over up trains.

10.55   A4 60024 KINGFISHER, down fast, 9.0 Kings Cross-Edinburgh.

10.58   V2 60950, up fast, 8.41 Hull-Kings Cross (running late, loco out of condition).

11.3   V2 60915 on 8.20 Harrogate-Kings Cross (13 coaches) due 10.50, left 11.9 after 60915 had handed over to another engine, then to shed.

11.11   A4 60020 GUILLEMOT 7.50 Newcastle-Kings Cross (due 11.4) delayed at outer home by above train. Departed 11.17 after 60020 had come off and to shed.

11.13   A1 60133 POMMERN, down fast, 'The White Rose' 9.10 Kings Cross-Leeds.

11.21   B1 61158 arrived two minutes late with 10.12 Doncaster-Grantham local (four coaches).

11.26   A4 60003 ANDREW K. McCOSH, down fast, 'The Norseman', 9.30 Kings Cross-Newcastle (Tyne Commission Quay); A1 60146 PEREGRINE off shed.

11.36   A3 60062 MINORU, up fast, 9.10 Hull-Kings Cross.

11.50   A3 60050 PERSIMMON, 9.5 Harrogate-Kings Cross.

Following on ABOYEUR's departure north an up fast to Kings Cross, the 8.10am departure from Leeds, runs through Grantham behind 60008 DWIGHT D. EISENHOWER. This A4 would be seen again at Grantham on the return journey from York. Photograph L.R. Freeman, The Transport Treasury.

You'll Remember those Black and White Days...

At the north end of Grantham station, with its three short sidings (a subway ran under the line at this point) a Thornaby V2, 60915, runs in at just after 11 o'clock with the thirteen coaches from Harrogate to Kings Cross. Within six minutes it had handed over to another engine and was off to shed. Photograph L.R. Freeman, The Transport Treasury.

By the time 60050 had arrived at 11.50, I was on my way again for at 11.37 A4 60023 GOLDEN EAGLE arrived three minutes early with the 9.40 Kings Cross-Newcastle, loaded to 12 corridors of which the leading four with 'Commonwealth' bogies were for Tyne Commission Quay. The start was a good one and 60023 ran as the log shows below. I should remark that the weather, which had been good, was now deteriorating with strong westerly winds and rain. As we left Grantham the wind set our exhaust rolling away to the east as we sped along to Retford. An unforgettable sight was to look forward to GOLDEN EAGLE as she so effortlessly, it seemed, rounded the curves in the storm. By Bawtry, the sun was out again but dark clouds loomed ahead. However, it was fairly dry at York. *The adjacent tables give the timings.*

We arrived a minute early to the screams of delight of many small boys; indeed, York station was full of them, of all ages and sizes including a few more elderly ones like myself. Incidentally, our engine had produced yelps of delight from

Miles		Min	Secs	Speed
0.0	Grantham (punctual start 1146)	0	00	
4.2	Barkston South Junction	6	42	60mph before pws
6.0	Hougham	8	57	
9.9	Claypole	12	42	60mph
14.6	Newark	18	40	MP116=71mph then pws
20.8	Carlton	25	22	MP124=58mph
25.8	Dukeries Junction	30	10	MP135=66mph
33.1	Retford	36	54	slight easing
38.4	Ranskill	41	49	Scrooby 67mph then pws
42.2	Bawtry (lively attack on 1 in 198)	47	16	surmounted 38mph
45.8	Rossington (dead stand for signals at Balby Jct and slipped slightly restarting)			
50.5	Doncaster	62	50	
	Arksey	65	32	
54.7	Shaftholme Junction	67	50	58mph to Jct/MP162=65
	Moss	70	22	
60.5	Balne	73	12	67mph
64.3	Templehurst	76	28	MP172=72mph
68.8	Selby (severe restriction for bridge)	80	27	
72.9	Riccall	85	40	
80.7	Chaloners Winn Junction	93	7	
82.6	York	96	52	

'spotters' further up the line, notably at Newark; GOLDEN EAGLE was a Gateshead locomotive and not very often to be seen, south of York at any rate. Observations between Grantham and York were as below.

Leaving Grantham: A3 60076 GALOPIN coming off shed.
Near Newark: A1 60145 SAINT MUNGO on up train.
Tuxford: B1 61171 on down goods in

the loop.
Retford: 9F 92174 on a down goods and B1 61126.
Bawtry Viaduct: A1 60118 ARCHIBALD STURROCK with up 'Yorkshire Pullman'.
Bawtry: B1 61003 GAZELLE in yard, and A3 60059 TRACERY up train.
Black Carr Junction: B1 61170 on down goods.
Doncaster in the yards and near the shed: V2s 60826 and 60917, B1 61194

Our reporter mentioned the demolition and loss going on at many of the stations north of Hitchin – this was the scene at Arlesey and Tempsford a few months before.

and 61314, O4/1 63693 and O2 63968; in the Works yard J50s Departmental No.10 and 68917; around the station A3 60036 COLOMBO, Britannia 70030 WILLIAM WORDSWORTH and B1 61223 on trains, and also K1 62069.

At York my hope, expressed earlier, was to see some North Eastern locomotives. Unfortunately, the J72 station pilots had just previously been replaced by small diesels but, as will be seen below, I was

successful in that some B16 4-6-0s that I had always wanted to see, put in an appearance. I did not leave the station, with its vaulting roof and curving platforms for I was, after all, only there for two hours.

Brighter times. St Neots near the time of Leslie Freeman's trip.

You'll Remember those Black and White Days...

60020 GUILLEMOT (arrives after a delay at the outer home) with a train from Newcastle. The Gateshead A4 then came off its train and went to shed to prepare for the return north. Photograph L.R. Freeman, The Transport Treasury.

Most of the time was spent at the north end and during my stay I observed Class 5 44861 and K3 61814, and B1 61086 leaving on a down train as I arrived. 44697 (with self-weighing tender) left on a south-bound train and Jubilee 45698 MARS was on the 10.30am Liverpool Exchange to York. Britannia 70030 followed 60023 from Doncaster with the 7.15am Colchester to Newcastle, then went on shed. A4 60028 WALTER K. WHIGHAM was on an up fast which I believe to have been the 9.45am Edinburgh Waverley to Kings Cross. Pacifics 60524 HERRINGBONE and 60103 FLYING SCOTSMAN followed, then B1 61018 GNU on a Scarborough train; V2 60966 was on a Kings Cross to Edinburgh service, V2 60968 arrived

B1 4-6-0 61158 rattles in two minutes late at 11.21am with a four coach Doncaster-Grantham local. Photograph L.R. Freeman, The Transport Treasury.

Miles		Min	Secs	Speed
0.0	York	0	00	
1.9	Chaloner's Whin Junction	4	15	
4.1	Naburn	6	43	MP180=73mph
9.6	Riccall	11	30	
13.7	Selby	15	35	slowing for pws
18.3	Templehurst	21	20	MP168=61mph
22.1	Balne	24	55	MP165=70mph
27.9	Shaftholme Junction	29	51	eased
	Arksey	32	13	
32.1	Doncaster	34	45	
34.9	Black Carr Junction	38	00	MP150=63mph
40.4	Bawtry	43	15	severe sig restriction
44.2	Ranskill	48	59	MP142=67mph
49.5	Retford	54	12	58mph up to Askhom tnl
	Dukeries Junction	60	45	MP128=75mph
68.2	Newark	70	55	Claypole 70/72mph
78.4	Barkston	81	1	pws
82.6	Grantham	87	15	

on the 11.30am Peterborough North to Edinburgh Waverley which went forward behind A3 60080 DICK TURPIN and 44781 arrived from the south, came off and was replaced by V2 60868. The V2 then stormed out with the train to Scarborough. B16/3 61476 went to shed, A3 60053 SANSOVINO passed on the up 'Northumbrian', 1.56pm off York, B1 61382 arrived from the north followed by A1 60129 GUY MANNERING, slipping badly on an up train.

A4 60003 ANDREW K. McCOSH seen earlier passing Grantham with the down 'The Norseman' came light from the shed, having obviously come off at York. A2/3 60516 HYCILLA then appeared on the up 'Norseman'; B1 61002 IMPALA ran light through the station and Britannia 70000 BRITANNIA came

off shed, also B1 61139 and 9F 92172. A1 60138 BOSWELL was on the 10.40am Kings Cross to Newcastle, arriving at 2.40pm and departing 2.50pm against booked times of 2.29pm and 2.37pm. A3 60085 MANNA was on up train which I believe to have been 'The Northumbrian'; Moguls 42931 and 42723 arrived from the north on a horse-van train and Britannia 70030 WILLIAM WORDSWORTH came off shed to work the 3.15pm York to Cambridge. V2 60918 arrived twelve minutes late at 2.52pm with 10.28am Kings Cross to Scarborough, replaced by B16/3 61472 which continued with the train at 3.7pm. Ivatt 4 43014 came off shed and A3 60084 TRIGO arrived on the 'Bristol side' with a train the details of which eluded me.

My train back to London, the 2.10pm Scarborough to Kings Cross, arrived, brought in by B16/3 61449 which promptly came off to be replaced by A3 60065 KNIGHT OF THE THISTLE. I had decided to travel on it because, apart from one short journey from Essendine to Peterborough, I had not journeyed behind an A3 before. As I boarded the train I was able to note 2-10-0 92170, Black Fives 44891 and 44823 double-heading a train in the far bay and V2 60808 waiting to follow us out with a down train. To return to my Scarborough train; it had come in late behind 61449 and 60065 set off for the next stop at Grantham at 3.24pm, fourteen minutes late. The log I give below. The exit from the station was cautious, then the A3 was set to work. The load, I think, was about 10 or 11 corridors. *See table above left.*

After such a fine run, I was disappointed when I found her being uncoupled at Grantham, but a glance ahead disclosed a corridor tender waiting to back down; it belonged to A4 60015 QUICKSILVER, so I was mollified. KNIGHT OF THE THISTLE had improved on the schedule by almost ten minutes so our arrival was only four minutes late. Engine changing took eight minutes instead of the booked five,

And so to York, reached through the eye of the storm. The rain has cleared enough to bring out once again the platform hordes. Photograph L.R. Freeman, The Transport Treasury.

You'll Remember those Black and White Days...

70000 BRITANNIA coming round from the shed at the north end of the station (that's part of the shed building on the left) ready to work a train southwards and home. Photograph L.R. Freeman, The Transport Treasury.

so QUICKSILVER set off for Kings Cross seven minutes late. However, with 122 minutes allowed for the 105 miles non-stop, it appeared that with some fair running we would be on time. So it proved, although 60015 was not perhaps in as good a mechanical condition as her external cleanliness suggested. She had a badly blowing gland so our progress was marked by a continuous 'phut-phut-phut' which seemed to get worse as we neared London. Still, apart from wasting water, it probably had little effect on

her performance. *See table below.* Once again the schedule had been improved on by almost ten minutes and final arrival was a shade over two minutes early, despite the stand for signals at Belle Isle box. Perhaps neither locomotive put up exceptional performances but I have given both logs in detail as they show the sort of work they did on ordinary trains, not just the 'flyers'. It also shows the operating side in a good light, with just one signal check, and that when we were running early. So far as the run was concerned, the

log speaks for itself I think, except that the crew overdid things a bit on Langley troughs and gave the leading coach a good wash!

Locomotives noted en route from York:
Doncaster (around station and yards): A4 60013 DOMINION OF NEW ZEALAND, A1 60122 CURLEW, A2/3 60520 OWEN TUDOR, B1s 61004 ORYX, 61087, 61128, 61141 and 61289, K3s 61871 and 61945, K1s 62053 and 62069, O2 63927, Ivatt 4 43154 and WD 90003.

Bawtry: B1 61003 GAZELLE on down light goods.
Scrooby: O4/8 63655 shunting in large yard.
Grantham: A4 60008 DWIGHT D. EISENHOWER arriving and O2 63941 on shed.
High Dyke: V2 60942 on up goods.
Stoke box: V2 60956 on down train.
Peterborough North: B1 61207, 9F 92042 and N2s 69504 and 69583.
Yaxley: 9F 92182 on up goods.
Arlesey: WD 90600 on up goods in Layly siding.
Hitchin: WD 90502.
Harringay: N2 69593 on up light goods.
Kings Cross: A1 60128 BONGRACE, A4s 60028 WALTER K. WHIGHAM' and 60033 SEAGULL and V2 60853, the latter two on arrivals.

Miles		Min	Secs	Speed
0.0	Grantham	0	00	
4.2	High Dyke	7	37	
5.4	Stoke	9	08	49mph
8.4	Corby Glen	12	00	MP96=78mph
16.9	Essendine	18	00	MP88=90mph
20.7	Tallington (psw near			
	Helpston)	20	36	88/89mph
29.1	Peterborough	31	00	severe restriction
36.1	Holme	39	32	70, to 62mph at summit
45.6	Huntingdon North	48	35	74/75mph
49.5	Offord	51	00	MP54=71mph
53.8	St Neots	54	50	pws
58.0	Tempsford	59	50	MP45=66mph
61.4	Sandy	63	20	slowing
64.4	Biggleswade	67	18	MP38=55mph
68.5	Arlesey	71	52	MP33=57mph
73.6	Hitchin	76	58	
76.9	Stevenage	80	40	MP26=61mph
80.5	Knebworth	84	05	
85.2	Welwyn Garden City	88	24	MP19=70mph
87.8	Hatfield	90	40	MP15=56/57mph
92.8	Potters Bar	95	40	
	Hadley Wood	97	59	
96.3	New Barnet	99	20	eased
	New Southgate	-	-	66mph
100.5	Wood Green	102	58	
103.0	Finsbury Park	105	25	
	Belle Isle	108	14	signal stop
105.5	Kings Cross	112	45	

A main point of the trip was to see such NER locomotives as remained in action. Thwarted by the replacement of the J72 station pilots by diesel shunters, compensation came in the form of several B16 4-6-0s. 61472 took over from V2 60918, taking forward the 10.28am Kings Cross-Scarborough. Photograph L.R. Freeman, The Transport Treasury.

Another B16, 61449, arrives with the Kings Cross train from Scarborough, to be boarded for the journey home by Leslie Freeman. The B16 promptly came off to be replaced by A3 60065 KNIGHT OF THE THISTLE. The A3's presence made the decision for our reporter, for one of his main intents had been to ride behind an A3. A marvellous day despite the rain! Photograph L.R. Freeman, The Transport Treasury.

You'll Remember those Black and White Days...

Four A1s at Kings Cross...

60131 OSPREY ready to depart Platform 6 at Kings Cross with the 'West Riding' on 18 May 1956. OSPREY was a GN A1 for all but the last year or so of its life; it spent most of the 1950s working from Copley Hill and on this occasion was only a couple of weeks out of Doncaster after a General. Three of the Leeds shed's A1s had been in works, making for a severe shortage of Pacifics there; things got worse when, a few weeks before this picture was taken, an over-taxed 60117 BOIS ROUSSEL of the depleted Copley Hill fleet dropped its brick arch in full flight. Photograph Frank Hornby.

Another GN stalwart, 60130 KESTREL glints in the sun at Kings Cross shed, 16 April 1962. It had been a Copley Hill engine since 1957. Photograph Peter Groom.

Long familiar in these columns, 60114 W.P. ALLEN at the Cross, in the early 1960s to judge from the electrification flashes and AWS. A splendid example of that 'rara avis', the matriarchal BR lady cleaner, takes a dim view of something. Photograph Peter Coster.

60149 AMADIS, come to a halt in Platform 6 in the early 1950s. It was one of the celebrated Grantham A1s, a link of six double-manned examples which each worked a diagram for two weeks, first with one crew, then with the other. Of the six, four worked to Kings Cross and back and two worked north of their home shed. Photograph A.J. Pike, O.B.E., Frank Hornby Collection.

Four A2s in Scotland...

Times had changed by 1962, with East Coast Pacific working in its last full year – it would end south of Peterborough the following year. On 2 June 1962 A2 60537 BATCHELOR'S BUTTON arrives at Berwick-on-Tweed with the 6.50am slow ex-Edinburgh Waverley. One of Haymarket's best throughout the 1950s, it had only late the previous year gone to St Margarets, as the diesels took over at Haymarket. The platform has a large number of pigeon baskets, the furthest lot with their doors open. Photograph Michael Mensing.

60539 BRONZINO on the up 'North Briton' approaches Berwick-on-Tweed on 1 June 1962. This A2 had a similar recent history to BATCHELOR'S BUTTON; it too had been ousted from a famous shed (Heaton) by diesels late in 1961 after spending the 1950s there. It had been a Tweedmouth engine since October 1961. Photograph Michael Mensing.

Not so much elegance of any sort in evidence at St Margarets shed on 2 August 1962. At Haymarket more or less since building, 60534 IRISH ELEGANCE was another victim of dieselisation, ousted at the end of 1961. It was condemned at the end of 1962. Photograph Peter Groom.

Before the general decline that was made so obvious by the end of 1961, 60530 SAYAJIRAO (later celebrated for its prolonged survival at Dundee) stands at Glasgow Queen Street on 13 May 1961. It had been at Haymarket for the great part of its life and it too would have to move on towards the end of the year. Photograph Michael Mensing.

You'll Remember those Black and White Days...

And Two of Each

SAYAJIRAO again, at Haymarket on 12 August 1960. Dieselisation was proceeding apace, the first part of the shed, suitably adapted, having gone over to the new order from the end of February – yet even at that late time there were still ten or more ex-NB locos present. Photograph Peter Groom.

Yet another Copley Hill A1, 60120 KITTIWAKE, on an up express about 1962. It has just crossed the Nene bridges south of Peterborough, while an EE Type 3 heads north with the down 'Master Cutler' Sheffield Pullman. Photograph Barry Richardson.

The end of an A2. New England, 2 June 1963 and a mournful 60533 HAPPY NIGHT stands abandoned in mid-repair. The decision was taken not to proceed and just thirteen days later it was withdrawn, after being carefully put back together again! Photograph Peter Groom.

An A1 brought low, 60129 GUY MANNERING on an up unfitted freight entering Berwick-on-Tweed on 22 May 1962. It was not condemned until late 1965. An Ivatt 2MT shunts on the left. Photograph Michael Mensing.

You'll Remember those Black and White Days...

Stanley's Pairings

Two locos await 'the go' at Southampton, apparently with trains for the LMR, in the early 1960s. The routing codes are held on by string, ingeniously utilising lamp irons and so on; it has a makeshift air though this would have been lost on the spotters chatting with the Fireman of the BR 2-6-0 or the lad shielding his ears from DORCHESTER's shrieking safety valves. Photograph Stanley Creer, The Transport Treasury.

Bishop's Stortford in June 1957, looking south as K3 61890 brings in a train for Cambridge, alongside light engine B2 61615 CULFORD HALL. Photograph Stanley Creer, The Transport Treasury.

Uproar in Belle Isle, under the high North London bridge, on 4 October 1958. The N2 69524 (first emblem) is presumably coming out ready to run down to Kings Cross for a suburban working; the N7 69654 (second emblem) is already on the way to Hatfield, with the 8.50am. Photograph Stanley Creer, The Transport Treasury.

One more pairing: Saltley's Fowler 2-6-4T 42421 at Platform 9, Birmingham New Street, with a Redditch train in March 1962, ready to leave behind the diesel shunter, 'parked up' during a pause in working. Photograph Stanley Creer, The Transport Treasury.

You'll Remember those Black and White Days...

LUMBERING GIANTS
The LNW Eight-Coupled Tanks
'She proceeded to straighten out the curves to suit her'
Ian Sixsmith, from original notes by Edward Talbot

The seventh 0-8-2T, 1592, fully lined out and with LNWR on the tank sides, at Willesden in 1922. This was part of the first batch of ten; the second two batches (of ten each) had the LNWR but were in plain black. The engine was in essence a tank version of the 'new G' 0-8-0. Buffers are the larger standard 'Webb' ones; there are locos with the earlier Cooke buffers either side of 1592.

The LNWR had relatively few engines specifically for shunting and with increasing demands as the 'gravity' method of working yards increased, something larger and more powerful was called for. In 1911 the LNW CME, C.J. Bowen Cooke, brought forth a new design of 0-8-2T based on the 0-8-0 tender engine of the previous year, the 'new G'. Practically, it was a tank version of the 'G' class, with rear pony truck supporting the coal bunker and a few minor alterations to make it more suitable for shunting. Boiler pressure was increased from 160lb to 170lb psi in the process, giving a greater reserve of power for short periods of heavy working. The rear tube plate was recessed into the boiler to make a combustion chamber with tubes at 13ft 4in (as in the 'A' and 'B' class compounds) instead of the 14ft of the 'G' class. Firebox heating surface and overall dimensions remained the same.

That this boiler was so modified for the 0-8-2Ts has been questioned in the past but confirmation comes in the lower tube heating surface shown both on the weight diagram and in several official lists of dimensions. Moreover there also exists a letter signed by Stanier, confirming the modification in response to an enquiry. Stanier wrote that the same boiler was used on the 0-8-2 tanks *'as on the 0-8-0 'D', 'F' and 'G' classes, with minor modifications, the most important being decreasing the distance between the tubeplates from 14ft to 13ft 4in, this accounting for the decreased heating surface, the barrel remaining the same in all cases, 14ft 6in'.* Standard 'G' class boilers had the same overall

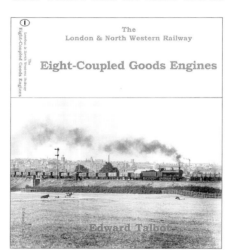

The
London & North Western Railway

Eight-Coupled Goods Engines

Edward Talbot

dimensions and in later days *were* fitted when no special boilers were available. This is quite clear from the Engine History Cards – when a boiler was fitted, the engine it came from is recorded too. New round-top boilers built as replacements were still being fitted, however, as late as 1931, though whether they were

special 0-8-2T boilers or standard 'G' class boilers is not clear.

The valve gear was also modified slightly. Valve travel was lengthened to make starting easier and a lever reverser, much more suitable for a shunting engine, was fitted. This was much more practical than the screw reverser fitted to all Crewe engines since its invention by Ramsbottom and introduction on his 'DX' class all the way back in 1858.

The 0-8-2T had one other difference of note from the standard 'G' class – though the engine itself had steam brakes, it was also fitted with vacuum brake for vacuum fitted wagons or passenger stock. The first 0-8-0 tender engines to be built with vacuum-brake equipment were to be the 'G1s' of 1914. Otherwise the big new tank had the standard 'G' class arrangements – three coupling rods (centre one fitted outside the other two), sandboxes on the two leading splashers, plus one either side under the cab and Instanter couplings.

***

Ten 0-8-2Ts were built over the two years 1911-1912, appearing in fully lined livery with 'LNWR' in twelve inch letters on the tank sides. Ten more were built in 1915 and another ten in 1916-1917. The second and third batches came out in plain black

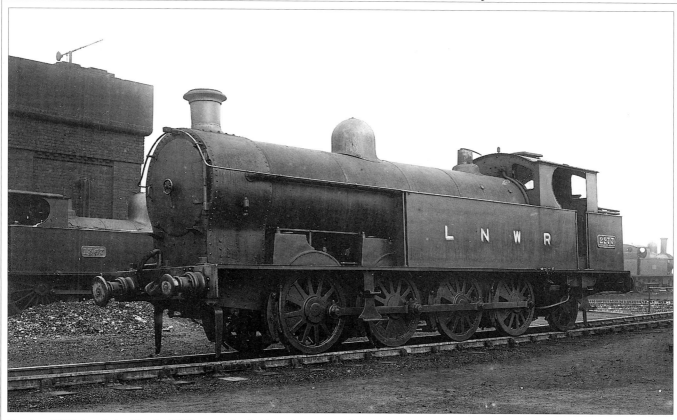

Engine 2277 in plain black, Hillhouse shed; Ramsbottom safety valves, two washout plugs on firebox side.

but still with 'LNWR' on the tank sides.

The 0-8-2Ts were widely used across the LNWR system and could be found at work in most of the larger yards. In 1913 *The Railway Magazine* reported that 'most' of them were working 'in the large sorting sidings at Crewe'. Three, 289, 482 and 2105, were at Blaenavon in August 1919; they later went to Patricroft, Willesden and Springs Branch respectively. Abergavenny had 1494 in August 1919. By 1928, they seem to have moved away from Crewe South and sheds where they could be found for many years included Willesden, Springs Branch, Speke Junction, Patricroft, Swansea, Bescot, Nuneaton, Huddersfield and Buxton. They are also known to have been allocated at times to Stafford, Shrewsbury and Rugby. The Willesden engines were occasionally used in emergency in the event of failures on up expresses. In this way 1514 and 1515 both managed to appear at Euston. On one occasion 1090 passed Watford on an up express,

No.1185 in an odd condition about 1923. Talbot considers the paintwork to have been touched up; the letters on the tank have been (imperfectly) 'touched out'.

0-8-2Ts

Crewe Wks No	LNWR No	Date Built	LMS No	Date Applied	Allocation at 1927	BR No	Date Applied	With-drawn
5040	1185	12/11	7870	05/28	Swansea			12/45
5041	1665	12/11	7872	06/26	Patricroft			10/36
5042	(1790	12/11						
	(r/n 1548	12/11	7871	08/28	Patricroft			05/35
5043	289	01/12	7873	08/28	Patricroft			01/35
5044	1163	01/12	7874	02/26	Patricroft			06/35
5045	1494	01/12	7875	10/26	Speke Jn	(47875)	n/a	08/48
5046	1592	01/12	7876	04/28	Speke Jn			07/47
5047	1659	01/12	7877	02/28	Speke Jn	47877	05/48	02/53
5048	1663	01/12	7878	11/26	Willesden			06/47
5049	2013	02/12	7879	09/27	Willesden			12/36
5247	58	08/15	7882	12/27	Willesden			10/34
5248	482	08/15	7880	06/27	Willesden			03/37
5249	563	08/15	7881	02/28	Willesden	47881	09/48	07/51
5250	736	08/15	7883	09/25	Stafford			03/35
5251	1090	09/15	7884	09/25	Rugby	47884	10/48	06/51
5252	1124	09/15	7885	07/26	Carnforth	(47885)	n/a	03/50
5253	1414	09/15	7886	05/28	Carnforth	(47886)	n/a	03/46
5254	1514	09/15	7887	11/27	Nuneaton	(47887)	n/a	08/48
5255	1515	09/15	7888	08/26	Huddersfield	(47888)	n/a	12/48
5256	2277	09/15	7889	04/28	Shrewsbury			10/34
5357	241	2/16	7890	09/26	Shrewsbury			06/39
5358	92	12/16	7891	08/27	Shrewsbury			06/46
5359	714	01/17	7892	08/25	Springs Branch	(47892)	n/a	02/48
5360	1291	01/17	7893	08/28	Springs Branch			10/34
5361	1331	01/17	7894	02/28	Springs Branch			09/39
5362	2105	01/17	7895	10/25	Springs Branch			10/34
5363	2294	01/17	7896	06/28	Buxton	47896	06/48	11/50
5364	2341	02/17	7897	04/28	Buxton			06/46
5365	2348	02/17	7898	06/27	Buxton			01/46
5366	2391	02/17	7899	01/28	Buxton			08/35

0-8-4Ts

Crewe Wks No	'LNWR' No	Date Built	LMS No	Date Applied	BR No	Date Applied	With-drawn	Notes
5722	380	02/23	7930	07/28	(47930)	n/a	08/48	
5723	782	02/23	7931	12/27	47931	11/48	12/51	
5724	1189	02/23	7932	06/28	(47932)	n/a	09/49	
5725	1677	02/23	7933	02/28	(47933)	n/a	06/50	
5726	1976	03/23	7934	08/28			05/46	
5727	256	03/23	7935	02/28			09/46	
5728	731	04/23	7936	05/28	(47936)	n/a	06/49	
5729	739	04/23	7937	04/28	47937	02/49	10/50	
5730	1908	04/23	7938	08/28	(47938)	n/a	02/48	
5731	1956	04/23	7939	08/26	(47939)	n/a	12/50	
5732	468	06/23	7940	08/28			01/46	
5733	792	06/23	7941	07/26			12/46	
5734	793	06/23	7942	06/26			11/44	
5735	(1904)	06/23	7943				02/47	(a)(b)
5736	(609)	06/23	7944				11/47	(a)
5737		08/23	7945				09/46	
5738		08/23	7946				12/47	
5739		08/23	7947				08/44	
5740		09/23	7948		(47948)	n/a	07/48	
5741		09/23	7949				10/46	
5742		10/23	7950				06/46	
5743		10/23	7951		(47951)	n/a	01/49	
5744		10/23	7952				08/45	
5745		10/23	7953				05/45	
5746		10/23	7954		(47954)	n/a	10/48	
5747		10/23	7955				08/46	
5748		11/23	7956		(47956)	n/a	11/48	
5749		11/23	7957				12/45	(b)
5750		11/23	7958		(47958)	n/a	12/48	
5751		01/24	7959		(47959)	n/a	6/48	

r/n = renumbered
(a) 7943 and 7944 were initially allocated 'LNWR' numbers 1904 and 60 respectively, but these were not carried.
(b) 7957 became 27957 in error in April 1934 but carried this number for a few days only. 7943 became 27943 (permanently) in 1945.

having probably hauled it from as far off as Rugby.

In 1928 the LMS allocation was as follows:

No	Shed	No	Shed
7870	Swansea	7887	Nuneat'n
7871-4	Patricroft	7888	Huddf'ld
7875-7	Speke Jct	7889-90	Shr'bury
7878-82	Willesden	7891	Rugby
7883-4	Stafford	7892-5	S. Branch
7885-6	Bescot	7896-9	Buxton

The engines moved around slightly soon after but the sheds operating the engines remained the same. In 1939 7892 was at Abergavenny but soon afterwards went to the North West. In the autumn of 1944 7888 was at Birkenhead for a short while.

Engine 7877 ran 20,104 miles in 1933 and 20,957 in 1936 but only 7,113 in 1930, 1,456 in 1931 and 9,279 in 1932. The reason for such low figures are obvious – these were the years of the Great Slump, when manufacturing, particularly in areas like the North West, experienced something like a collapse. Shunting engines such as these were needed less and less and spent many months in store 'awaiting better economic conditions'. 7877 was allocated to Speke from March 1928 but went to Edge Hill in July 1932. In times of better traffic, from 1937 to 1950, it averaged well over 20,000 miles a year, reaching a high of 30,472 in 1946. In June that year it was transferred back to Speke. Even in 1950, when it was scrapped, it ran 17,081 miles. Its total mileage was 701,005.

The mileage figures for 7881 are closely similar, 692,706. An engine that avoided the low returns of 1929-32 was 7884, even though it transferred from Willesden to Speke in October 1929 and from there to Springs Branch in June 1930. Its highest annual mileage was 30,531 in 1942 and the total when scrapped as 47881 in 1951 was 732,425. No.7885 at Bescot ran only 580 miles in 1930 and was out of service for no less than 271 days (263 stored, 3 not required and 5 under repair on shed). Its total mileage was 553,433, while 7896 managed a haul of 715,830.

There were few alterations made to the 0-8-2Ts. The first batch had the then-standard long-taper Bowen-Cooke buffers but they must have proved unsuitable in some way – possibly they were not robust enough to withstand the constant buffering up to and pushing of heavy loads or perhaps the heads were just too small and led to buffer-locking on sharp curves in yards. At any event they were soon replaced by the standard large 18 inch Webb buffers. The second and third batches seem to have had these buffers from new. Engines used at Garston Docks had

You'll Remember those Black and White Days...

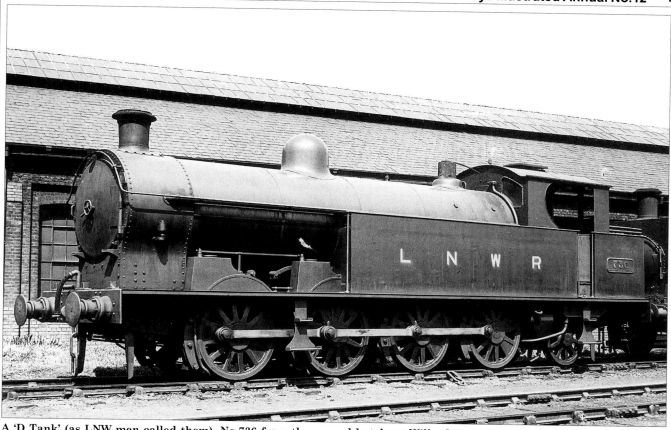

A 'D Tank' (as LNW men called them), No.736 from the second batch, at Willesden in 1921.

to be fitted with 'wooden buffer blocks' according to the general arrangement drawing. This would perhaps be the explanation for the wooden 'pads' on 7880 – see picture. The precise reason is not known. In LMS days standard parallel-sided LMS buffers were used as replacements for the Webb type.

All engines had plain top chimneys but at least one is known to have borne a capuchon for a time, no doubt a replacement from a tender engine. In LMS days alterations were confined to standard LMS fittings, safety valves and lamp irons. Unlike the larger LNWR engines, both passenger and goods, no 0-8-2Ts ever had the cab roof cut back to the LMS composite loading gauge. None was ever superheated, nor were any fitted with Belpaire fireboxes. At some stage in LMS days the water filler in the bunker was raised in height, probably to allow water to be taken more easily when the bunker was well filled with coal or, more likely, to stop coal falling down into the tank! Some engines lost their vacuum brake equipment at this time. No doubt it had fallen into disrepair on some engines as it was rarely if ever needed in certain yards. Its removal was merely recognition of this.

Minor technical 'improvements' were very similar to those found on the 0-8-0 tender engines. In the period up to 1935 Midland type water gauges were fitted, along with

desanding apparatus. Ross pop safety valves replaced the Ramsbottom type, though it is possible that in one or two cases Ramsbottom valves later replaced pop valves once again. Ashblowers were removed, as were blow-off cocks, while an improved method of fitting the internal main steam pipes in the smokebox was adopted. Lubricators were removed from the boiler faceplates and some engines had receptacles fitted for spare gauge glasses.

No.7882, the first of the second batch and originally LNWR No.58, was the first of the 0-8-2Ts scrapped, in October 1934. Sixteen were still in service at the outbreak of the Second World War and all survived to its end; only ten were allotted BR numbers in 1948 and only four actually carried them. The last to be withdrawn was 47877 in February 1953. It had outlived the last of the 0-8-4Ts by some nineteen months.

***

The final LNWR eight-coupled engine and indeed the final LNWR class of any kind, was the 0-8-4T designed under the reign of H.P.M. Beames. No.380 actually appeared some months after the Grouping. In the usual manner, it was based on the latest 0-8-0 tender engine – in essence a 'G2' with a rear bunker, supported by a standard double radial truck, and side tanks. It had the same arrangement of coupling

rods, with the centre one pin-jointed to the outer ones and the same arrangement of sandboxes. Some detail changes there were: vacuum brakes, operated by two 24in diaphragm-type vacuum cylinders and a hand brake operating on the rear four coupled wheels only; steam-heating apparatus for working passenger trains; a chimney without a capuchon; anti-vacuum valves at the sides of the base of the smokebox and wire mesh on the rear widows as protection when coaling. The buffers were the parallel ones of the type which replaced the original buffers on the 0-8-2Ts. The buffer beam ends were shaped to provide clearance on curves in view of the additional 'throw-over' compared to the tender engine.

In all major respects, then, the new engine was a tank version of the 'G2'. Though it had a boiler pressure of 185lb psi instead of 175lb, it had the same frames, increased in thickness (from one inch) by an additional eighth of an inch. There were the same enlarged axleboxes, slide bars and horn blocks. The gudgeon pins were about an inch more in diameter than the 'G1s' and 'G2As', the cross heads were deeper in section to allow for the larger pins and the piston rods were of a larger diameter also. Of course, the reason for some of these changes was the need to provide for the extra weight of the water in the side tanks. All journals were lubricated from a Silvertown

Fading lettering on 2277; a change is the built-up water filler in the bunker, taking the lid clear of the coal (the join between the old filler and the new addition is clear). This illustrates clearly an odd feature of the eight coupled tanks; there was no filler – or, for that matter, a conventional breather – on the side tanks. This is the reason for the square-section connection under the running plate from the base of the rear tank to the rear of the side tank. This was so that water put in that rear filler could reach the side tanks. That said, there must have been some form of air escape ('breather') from the side tanks, which are not obvious from any photographs.

mechanical lubricator on the left-hand side, just ahead of the sandbox on the driving axle (the second one from the front). The cylinders and steam chests were served by a Wakefield hydrostatic lubricator in the cab. The injectors were standard LNWR-type Webb injectors, 9mm on the right and 11mm on the left. Water feeds were brass hand wheels on the top of the tanks.

The 0-8-2Ts had been built purely for shunting, but the 0-8-4Ts were intended for short-distance haulage of heavy trains, as in the South Wales coalfield. Many spent their lives there, where tender-first running in winter was particularly to be avoided. Coal and water capacity was 3½ tons and 2,030 gallons, compared with 2½ tons and 1,200 gallons in the 0-8-2Ts. Working in colliery areas still involved considerable shunting and

No.7880 with a background of brand-new Black Fives, at Crewe on 14 April 1935. Ramsbottom valves now replaced by Ross pop valves. The timber backings to the buffers, as yet unpainted, stand out for once. Photograph L. Hanson.

That fine upright quality shown to good effect at Edge Hill in the late 1930s. Target 45 would be one of the innumerable dock trips in the district. The engine now has LMS buffers and four washout plugs on the firebox side.

so a dual screw and reversing gear was fitted – the screw for adjusting cut-off and lever for quick reverse when shunting. It took up more room in the cab, precluding the fitting of a boiler with Belpaire firebox – so the engines always had the round-top variety. In fact, the reach rod was low down at the side of the firebox and it might have been possible to fit a Belpaire but the tanks took up a large area of the footplate, so that the driver would not have been able to look forward out of the cab. It was already difficult enough with the round-top boiler.

***

The well-known railwayman and author, J.M. Dunn, who started his career on the LNWR in 1913, wrote of the 0-8-4Ts both in his splendidly acerbic autobiography *Reflections on a Railway Career* (Ian Allan, 1966) and in an article in *The Railway Magazine* in April 1953. Based in South Wales by 1923, he engineered a visit to Abergavenny when the expectant rumours were at last confirmed – at last something larger than the lightly built 'Coal Tank' 0-6-2Ts would be available for work in the coal field. The first 0-8-4T, No.380, arrived at Abergavenny shed on 28 May 1923 and Dunn describes it thus: '*It was a beautiful evening and*

I well remember No.380 standing just outside the shed doors with the sun shining on its gleaming paintwork, which was in the full LNWR style but with one big difference. Instead of the letters LNWR on the tank sides, as was then the fashion with the big tank engines, the letters LMS appeared. It was the first engine I had seen bearing these initials and was in fact the first sign of any sort that I had seen, apart from headings on printed matter, of the momentous changes that had taken place in the railway world on the previous New Year's Day'

There was one other concession to the new company – LMS lamp irons were fitted in place of the usual LNWR sockets. Again, although the first engine had Ramsbottom safety valves, Ross pop safety valves were introduced very soon after, possibly on the second engine. Once again, thirty engines were built, in three batches of ten and all were turned out at the time when the LMS was deciding its new livery. Thus, they appeared in four different schemes, as detailed below:

LNWR lined black, LNWR numberplates, 'LMS' on tanks: 7930-7937
Plain black, LNWR numberplates, no lettering on tanks: 7938-7942
LMS 'crimson lake' with gold lining:* 7943-7948
LMS plain black: 7949-7959
*for passenger work around Abergavenny

The first seven followed Dunn's No.380 to Abergavenny on entering service, as did three of the following six. At first Nos.739, 468 and 793 were sent to Tebay where presumably they were tried on banking up to Shap. This seems not to have been successful, for they were soon transferred to Abergavenny. The next eleven, up to 7953, also went new to Abergavenny; the last six went to Edge Hill but may have gone to Abergavenny initially.

Soon after the class arrived at Abergavenny, trials were held with one – a load of 209 tons, consisting of thirty wagons and a 20-ton brake van, was started from rest on a ruling grade of 1 in 34 in bad weather. The load was increased to 392 tons and on a 1 in 40 these were taken with ease, and several more wagons could have been added but for the fact that a greater length of train was inadmissible on that section of line. In passenger service on 1 in 34 a train of fourteen vehicles was easily handled and the test was only not extended because the platforms could not accommodate more vehicles. The report concluded that the nineteen engines at work in the Abergavenny District were doing the work of thirty of the former 'Coal Tanks'. Some were sent to work between Manchester and Buxton,

One of the big shunting tanks in Crewe Works, 7892 on 14 June 1936. Photograph L. Hanson.

the idea being that one class of engine could work all traffic, both passenger and goods, as well as doing the shunting at Buxton. They were, of course, fine on goods trains and, no doubt, had better acceleration from the frequent stops when working uphill towards Buxton than either the 4-4-2 'Precursor Tanks', which had worked the line

from the mid-1900s, or the 4-6-2 'Superheater Tanks', which had replaced them about 1921. But with their small wheels they were less suitable for passenger work and were certainly not right for the express passenger trains. Eventually, a few years later, the Buxton services were taken over by Fowler 2-6-4Ts.

Published accounts show the engines used on the Buxton line as being allocated to Longsight; in July 1925, for instance, two of them, 7955 and 7956, are shown as sent there. According to the Engine History Card, 7932 was also at Longsight on 1 January 1927 (when the card starts) but was transferred to Edge Hill the following day; in November

Official view of the first 0-8-4T with the LNWR livery but otherwise with the 'LMS' that made such an impression on Dunn at Abergavenny in 1923.

A fine portrait of 7885 at Bescot, 17 March 1935. It still has the Cooke buffers, which is surprising given the late date, as well as Ramsbottom safety valves. This is one of the few pictures to reveal the curious slotted gap at the base of the smokebox behind the buffer beam – a feature of many LNW engines. It has the four washout plugs but retains the lower water filler. That looks like an oil, or maybe a water leak between the rear driver and the trailing wheel, coating the injector feed pipe in the process, while someone has gone for some sand by the look of it, leaving the filler lid on the sandbox.

of that year it went to Abergavenny. It is fairly certain that the 'Longsight' engines were actually working from Buxton. At that time it was a 'sub-shed' of Longsight under the LNWR shed organisation, and engines were officially recorded as being at the 'home' shed. The 0-8-2Ts, which had been moved away when the 0-8-4Ts arrived, returned to Buxton in late 1925.

In essence the engines were shared between two areas, Liverpool and South Wales, throughout their lives. In the 1928 LMS block allocations they were shedded as follows: 7930-7946 (five or six outstationed at Blaenavon) at Abergavenny; 7947-7948 at Swansea; 7949-7959 Edge Hill. These allocations remained thus for many years but some of the South Wales engines were moved around between Abergavenny, which always had the greatest number, Swansea and Tredegar. The Swansea ones also worked from Landovery as Sugar Loaf bankers.

The 0-8-4Ts had higher boiler pressure than the 'G2' 0-8-0s and greater adhesive weight, thanks to the side tanks. They were powerful engines and, vitally, enjoyed excellent braking. Yet they were still not popular with crews, who disliked the cramped and uncomfortable footplate. As the tanks protruded into the cab, the driver had to stand too near the fire, and as the firehole was low, the fireman had to bend low to shovel and then could easily hit his head on the handle of the rack-type firehole door. Wooden footblocks were fitted for the men to stand on but took up much of the floor space. These problems would not have existed if the tanks had been further forward and the footplating lowered.

The 0-8-4Ts' arrival in South Wales was ill-starred in that they tended to straighten out the track on a number of the sharper curves. This is hardly surprising in view of the fact that they were new, with a long rigid wheelbase. Dunn, confronted with No.380 in Abergavenny shed yard, looked somewhat askance at that long wheelbase and, sure enough, when it came to Tredegar the next day and was set to work, the trouble started: *'Apart from the long wheelbase she was new and 'tight' so that there was no play in her joints and she proceeded to straighten out the curves to suit her. The platelayers had to follow her round correcting the curves she had distorted'.* Dunn recalls a PW Department inquiry into the matter in October 1923 at which he suggested improving the flexibility of the big tank engines by substituting three short rods on each side for the long jointed coupling rods. The existing joints on the three rods (which were very robust) did not allow movement in the horizontal. He was informed that Crewe would be adopting this idea but nothing seems to have come of it. The GW became so concerned, it is said, that they banned the 0-8-4Ts from any part of their Rhymney line from March 1924. However, they were still working excursions at the top end between Rhymney Bridge and Rhymney into 1936.

Derailments were another problem. Consider these slightly hair-raising events: *'On 20 March 1929, No.7936 had one pair of bogie wheels derailed in Blaenavon goods yard and on 1 May No.7932 came off the road and blocked the entrance to the engine shed. Outside Blaenavon shed one of the two roads was on a curve and the flangeless wheels often used to become derailed there. When I first went to Blaenavon hardly a morning passed but I had to take jacks and packing to lift a pair of these wheels on the road again, but eventually I tired of it and, like the enginemen, took no notice. When the engine was ready to leave the shed they just started away with the*

The beast in its lair, 1920s. No.7953 down at Canada Dock, Liverpool, a branch off the Bootle branch and part of the LNW's spectacularly graded and engineered access to the vast Liverpool Docks. LMS smokebox numberplate (these were removed in the 1930s), number on tanks, 'LMS' on bunker sides, Liverpool Docks Target number; the first 0-8-4Ts, it seems, had the Ramsbottom safety valves, but most of the rest had the Ross pop valves, as here.

flangeless wheels bumping along the ground until they reached the first pair of points when there was a bigger bump and the wheels rerailed themselves without any trouble at all!

'In an endeavour to stop the [third pair of] flangeless wheels derailing at this place, I used to keep the rails well sanded and get the drivers to keep the brake blocks rubbing on the wheels while the engines were brought round the curve. This reduced the number of derailments considerably, but more than once I have seen the flangeless wheels slip sideways and fall off the rails as soon as the hand brake was released and before the engine started to move! No.7946 was a particular offender in this respect.'

There were darker tales of the 0-8-4Ts derailing while on the road, with drivers convinced that the flangeless wheels slipped off the rail

No.7942 around 1936. The shed is almost certainly Edge Hill. It was the third pair of wheels (from the front) that were flangeless, and they had wider treads.

and came back on again, to accompanying and alarming thumps and bangs. Dunn was never able to confirm this, but he did experience 'the most alarming thuds' when the engines were running. As he writes, 'there seemed no other explanation'.

Although there is no doubt that Dunn's problems were only too real, it remains something of a mystery as to how this could happen. There was no side play in these axleboxes at all and the treads of the wheels were wide, while the coupling rods to the neighbouring wheels were only 5ft 9in long. Even if the axleboxes had been free to move sideways, it is hard to imagine how they could do so, as the coupling rods should have restrained them. So it seems unlikely that they would derail in any normal circumstances and several drivers at Abergavenny, who were questioned about this in the early 1940s, could not recall an 0-8-4T ever derailing. Of course, all engines derail at times, and the big tanks must have been susceptible on all those poorly maintained colliery sidings but the flangeless driving wheels seem, on the face of it, no more likely to derail than any others. Though it may be difficult to explain how it happened, it nonetheless did! Similar things are known to have occurred at times with the flangeless wheels of 'Super Ds' and of BR 9F 2-10-0s.In the early

1940s Abergavenny had ten 0-8-4Ts; 7931-7932, 7935-7936, 7940, 7943-7945, 7947 and 7956. They ran colliery trips in the area and goods trains to Newport and Dowlais Central as well as banking from Monmouth Road to Llanvihangel. They served as bankers to Brynmawr and would then work to Blaina or Ebbw Vale, or shunt at Brynmawr, Beaufort and Rassau Siding. A handful of the Abergavenny engines were outstationed at Blaenavon (closed from 5 September 1942) on colliery work, taking the coal to Abergavenny. It was here that an 0-8-4T nearly brought Mr Dunn's career to a messy end... Blaenavon was a little two road dead-end shed with the offices at the rear, beyond the buffer stops. One dark night he was surprised by an agitated driver bursting in and shouting to 'come and see where we are!' Dunn stepped in the shed and followed the driver down to the yard. There, a few feet from two dead engines standing on the road facing the office door, was an 0-8-4T with twenty wagons of coal! The train had been coming down the single line goods loop and instead of going to the left through the station and on to Talywain went right, into the engine shed. The signalman had forgotten the train and had omitted to set the points for the main line and only the alert driver saved Mr Dunn.

Tredegar had four 0-8-4Ts in the early 1940s, 7933, 7937, 7939 and 7952 and worked them very hard; they did not spend much time idle on shed. The quartet served the collieries in the Sirhowy Valley, worked freight to Ystrad Mynach via Hengoed Viaduct and, after the war started, ran to Aber sidings, Caerphilly and Rogerstone yard. They also regularly worked passenger trains for miners, made up of wooden-seated four and six-wheeled carriages, between Nantybwch and Nine Mile Point colliery, with a banker from Tredegar to Nantybwch in the reverse direction. On Tuesdays they worked a special market train to Abergavenny, running non-stop from Sirhowy to Brecon Road in front of the 10am Merthyr-Abergavenny passenger and returning about 4.30pm. In the football season they worked to such places as Cardiff and Pontypridd and in the summer took excursion trains for Barry Island (probably coming off at Cardiff). They also worked rugby specials for Murrayfield from Pentllanfraith as far as Abergavenny, where main line engines would take them on.

Swansea Upper Bank, a former Midland shed, also had 0-8-4Ts in the 1940s, probably four. They were used on colliery trips in the Swansea valley area and brought the coal to sidings near St Thomas's

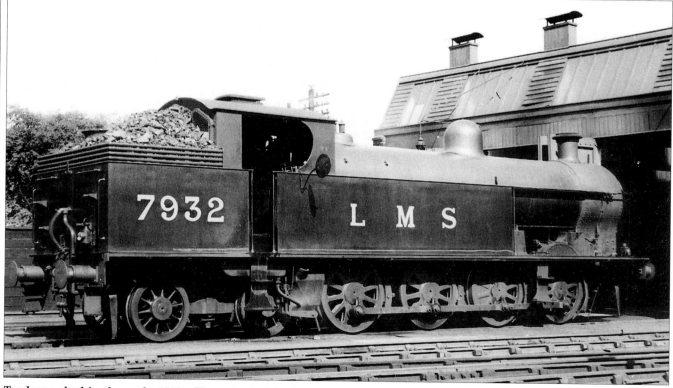

Tredegar shed in the early 1930s. The principal bugbear was the lubrication to the trailing driving axleboxes. Flexible oil pipes led from the mechanical lubricator and these were clipped to the main frame behind the wheels. When new, this arrangement caused no trouble but when side-play developed in the axlebox, the wheel eventually rubbed away at the pipe, causing loss of oil and overheating. Worse, the things were 'the very devil' to get at. It would have been possible to overcome this fault easily by re-routing the pipe but nothing was done. At Tredegar Mr Dunn was reduced to applying a mix of graphite and sulphur ('bought in the town'!) every night to avoid having to drop the wheels at Abergavenny.

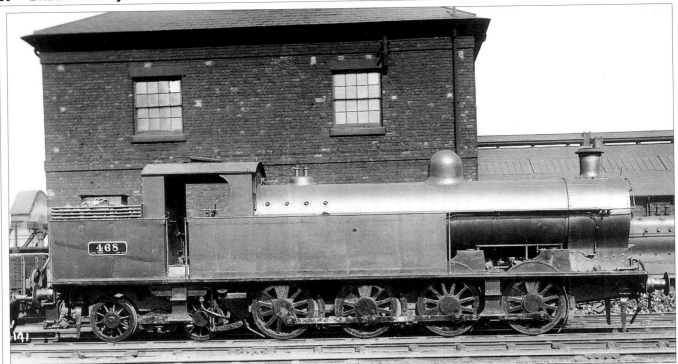

No.468 in fine fettle at Shrewsbury. The crosshead driven pumps were very neat arrangements but again, when sideplay developed, the fastening nuts fouled the axlebox and off came the studs. Sheds would very soon disconnect the pumps and they would stay that way until the engine next visited works.

station where it was handed over to the GWR. When the war started, they worked through over GWR metals. To reach Upper Bank they ran from Crewe via the Central Wales line to Swansea Victoria and then over the elevated line joining the east and west sides of Swansea docks.

Liverpool was the other great stronghold of the 0-8-4Ts. There they were used mostly on good workings on the branches to the docks. They worked trains from the branches to the top of the 'Grid Iron' and then ran back for another trip. They also worked local goods to Speke. The main reason for sending

them to Edge Hill seems to have been the working of the Bootle branch, both passenger and freight. Previously, the load limit for goods trains from Alexandra and Canada Docks was 31 wagons (figures actually vary) up the 1 in 63 from Atlantic Junction to Walton & Anfield. They were usually hauled by

No.7940 and crew pose for Mr Dunn at Blaenavon. When he arrived there in 1928 there were five 0-8-4Ts, 7938, 7939, 7940, 7941 and 7942, but with the Depression from the following year there were probably fewer engines involved. Four were out at work all day; three were re-manned while the fourth was only single manned and did not leave the shed until late morning. The fifth would be away at Abergavenny for washing out and was exchanged in traffic at Brynmawr on alternate days. Photograph J.M. Dunn, LNWR Society.

You'll Remember those Black and White Days...

Arriving at Manchester London Road with empty stock from Longsight, about 1925. No.7955 was one of the 0-8-4Ts tried out on the Manchester-Buxton trains.

a 'Cauliflower', '19in Goods' or 0-8-0 and were always banked, perhaps by a 'Coal Tank'. The 0-8-4Ts could take the whole train single-handed with ease, and the intention was to double the load. But the guards refused to take such heavy trains, as 31 wagons was the most a guard's van could hold on the banks. On passenger trains the big tanks were very quick in getting away from Lime Street up the cutting to Edge Hill. The 4pm to Bootle went up the bank parallel to the 4pm Leeds train and invariably the 0-8-4T won the 'race'. They also worked passenger trains to Alexandra Dock and Canada Dock via Atlantic Junction, and in doing so provided plenty of excitement for enthusiasts. When they began to be withdrawn, their work on the Bootle branch was taken by 'Super D' 0-8-0s.

The 0-8-4Ts generally seem to have been well liked at Edge Hill. There were familiar complaints – the firehole door was regarded as too low and with the rack type door, firemen were hitting their heads on the handle when firing. If both men were on the large side, the driver used to stand by the cab door out of the way when the fireman was at work. When he had finished firing, he often used to sit on the end of the tank and stretch his legs across the opening to the cab, while running light to Alexandra or Canada docks to pick up another load for Edge Hill. Hot boxes were not uncommon but in

general the problems of PW damage and derailing found in South Wales seem to have been absent. Why that should have been so is a minor mystery, for there were plenty of steep gradients and hard work in the dock area and around the 'Grid Iron'. Perhaps one factor was that the sharp curves in the docks were banned to main line engines and were worked by dock tanks of various kinds instead.

Allocations were not static but the following engines were at Edge Hill in 1938: 7943-7944, 7946, 7948, 7950,7953, 7955, 7957-7959. In 1947 it was: 7930, 7933,7938-7939, 7946, 7951, 7956, 7958-7959; in 1948: 7930-7933, 7937, 7939, 7951, 7956, 7958-7959. When Edge Hill engines were withdrawn, they were replaced by examples from South Wales but eventually 'Super D' 0-8-0s took over.

All the 0-8-4Ts went to Rugby Works for shopping. The South Wales ones got there via Shrewsbury, Wellington and Stafford. Occasionally they went via Crewe and South shed might borrow them when en route and sent them on a freight to Liverpool.

As regards mileages, 47931 had an annual tally between 1927 and 1936 which varied from a low of 11,912 in 1930 to a high of 19,228 in 1936, but between 1937 and 1950 its average was over 20,000 miles. A total of 25,409 was recorded in 1940 and 26,116 in 1942. It was allocated to Abergavenny from 1927 to

September 1942 and then to Swansea till February 1948, when it went to Edge Hill. Its total mileage when withdrawn was 522,542. No.7933 ran 26,585 miles at Swansea in 1943 and 26,060 at Abergavenny in 1946. In all, it ran 510,987 miles. No.7939 ran a total of 534,584 miles. In fact, it was difficult for engines in South Wales to run up high mileages, as their work was confined to either Abergavenny-Dowlais, about eighteen miles and Nantybwch-Newport via Tredegar, twenty-two miles. They did not go to Merthyr.

Changes in the external appearance of the 0-8-4Ts were few. LMS buffers began to be fitted, probably in the late 1930s, front numberplates were removed generally earlier than that. Anti-vacuum valves were removed from the sides of the base of the smokebox on some engines, though they remained in use on those at Abergavenny. Some engines can be seen in photographs running without carriage-heating hoses though this probably denotes summertime, when the apparatus was taken off for refurbishing. The distinctive LNWR cab roof remained unaltered, unlike most of the tender engines. Some got LMS 'Stanier' chimneys while, late on, some engines got conventional smokebox door handles instead of the LNW style 'wheels'.

Many minor technical changes occurred, especially in the 1923-

No.739, one of two to get a BR number, at Crewe South in the 1920s, shortly after its introduction; it still has the Ramsbottom safety valves.

1926 period, almost all of them the same as those carried out on the 'Super Ds'. Pop safety valves were fitted on the few that originally had Ramsbottom valves but in the early days at least, it is quite possible that, *vice versa* as it were, Ramsbottom valves replaced pop valves in some cases. The eight inch piston valves originally had one broad ring per head but were later fitted with four narrow rings. Midland type water gauges and desanding apparatus were also fitted. Ashblowers and blow off cocks in the door plates were lately removed. The improved method of fitting the main steam pipes in the smokebox was adopted and copper ejector steam pipes were used instead of steel, as were standard type cone unions* and continuous blowdown apparatus.

Crosshead-driven vacuum pumps appear to have been retained in many cases and ejectors added (only No.7931 has 'pump' crossed out on the History Card). One engine is recorded as having been provided with 'driver's seats', presumably improved seats for both members of the crew, and probably other engines were also so fitted.

The first engine to be withdrawn was 7947 in August 1944 and the rest of the class followed as their boilers required replacement. At first, when replacement boilers were fitted in the works, they had come from other 0-8-4Ts and had been repaired, but after about 1930 boilers previously on 'Super Ds' were fitted. When it became uneconomic to repair round-top boilers, replacements were no longer available, as all spare boilers built since the 1920s had had Belpaire fireboxes. So withdrawal was inevitable. Just over half of the class, sixteen, had been withdrawn by nationalisation in 1948 and of the fourteen which became BR property only two survived long enough to receive BR numbers, 47931 and 47937. The latter was withdrawn in October 1950 but the former survived for more than a year, until it was withdrawn in December 1951.

Finally, there is the question as to what the 0-8-4Ts sounded like. Did they have the same uneven beat as a 'Super D' or an even beat? Jack Gahan of Liverpool recalls them as sounding like a 'Super D' but when working flat out up 1 in 63 or on the 'Grid Iron' the beat was almost even. So the question was also put to Harold Walkley: 'Can you recall ever hearing these Beames tanks in action?' His reply was as follows: *'I noticed the 0-8-4Ts were permitted ten ICI 35-ton tank wagons unassisted into Abergavenny Junction whereas the 0-8-0s were restricted to nine. The way these trains were driven was like this. They would come down from Brynmawr with brakes pinned down (average grade 1 in 38 for 7½ miles) and stop at Llanfoist cutting to lift the brakes. When ready, the driver gave a coded whistle to Brecon Road No.2 box and when the signalman had a clear road to the junction, he would pull off the distant signal by the train and off they would set – full regulator, full gear, accelerating bunker first up the 1 in 60 through Brecon Road station, then the track eased to 1 in 90 where the driver would pull the lever back to the fourth notch. The noise was tremendous and each of the exhaust beats was even.'* 'Tremendous' would seem thoroughly apt...

The above notes are in parts a compression and in parts an expansion, together with extra photographs and tables, of the relevant sections of Edward Talbot's monumental book *The LNWR Eight Coupled Goods Engines*. With, of course, the author's full blessing. This book can hardly be more highly recommended for LNW/LMS enthusiasts; copies are available from all good specialist bookshops or from Mr Talbot (cheap at £30 plus 10% p&p for more than 250 high gloss art pages with brilliant photographic reproduction) at 32 Waterside Court, Gnosall, Stafford, ST20 0AR, et@team.u-net.com Any errors that may have crept into the above rendition are of course mine and nothing to do with the original author!

Thanks also to Bryan Wilson and Eric Youldon.

*'cone unions' recall a minor mystery, recently solved through further researches at Kew by Edward Talbot. The phrase 'coal unions' appears clearly on many History Cards and in the absence of clarification has been repeated so on a number of occasions. It turns out the clerk responsible for maintaining the cards at this period misread the notes, and so the error, 'coal unions', a minor historical dead end, was born. This sets the record straight!

No.7957 at Edge Hill in April 1934, the tank filler for once unobscured by heaped up coal.

No.7938 in the 1930s. It carries a 4D Abergavenny plate and that's almost certainly where it is. Just visible at the front right-hand corner of the cab roof is the carriage heating relief valve, fitted to the 0-8-4Ts as well as a few 'Super Ds'.

You'll Remember those Black and White Days...

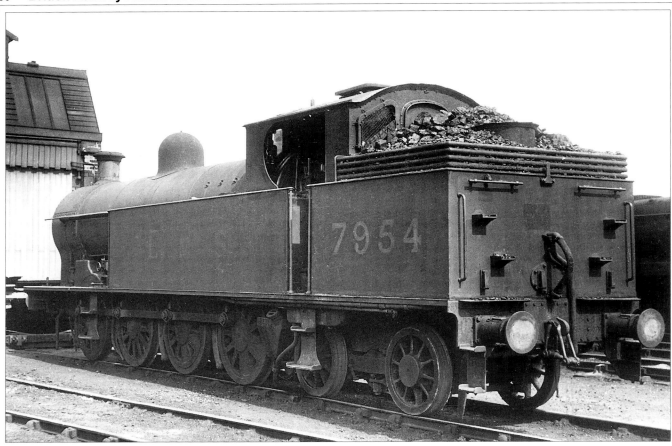

A down-at-heel 7954, with left-hand injector pipe partly dismantled, at the back of Buxton shed in August 1948. LMS buffers, four washout plugs. Photograph F.W. Shuttleworth.

7954 at Buxton during the terrible winter of 1947. It had had to be recovered from Briggs Siding where its crew had 'baled out' and abandoned it. The gentleman is the shed foreman, Joe Wilson. Photograph E.R. Morten.

A lively 7937, the last survivor withdrawn as 47937 in October 1950, at Edge Hill on 9 September 1948. Conventional smokebox door handle instead of LNW 'wheel'. Photograph F.W. Goudie, The Transport Treasury.

Back to the 0-8-2Ts again for a reminder of that architectural quality, on an otherwise shabby 7892. The background suggests Liverpool and the Grid Iron.

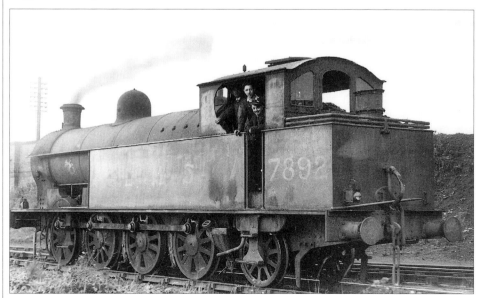

You'll Remember those Black and White Days...

THE WARTIME RAILWAY JOURNEYS OF JOHN AIRD

It's clearly impossible to illustrate the complex comings and goings of John Aird and his millions of compatriots during the Second World War. Even the official record of trains at work is threadbare at best and no soldier would dare to photograph troop movements even if he could afford a camera and film or was prepared to carry it around with all the other kit. Photography was in fact positively forbidden to a serving soldier and only a few chanced it – the late lamented Harold James for instance took a few covert shots of USA S160 2-8-0s from the camp perimeter at his RAF station but was aware the 'high jump' awaited if he was caught. Pre-eminent in the recollections of all who observed railways in the war are, overwhelmingly, the enormous loads. When John Aird saw EMPIRE OF INDIA on the 10.00am Waverley-Kings Cross, still named 'Flying Scotsman' and slowing for the Berwick stop with nineteen coaches in January 1942 it would have been in wartime black with the skirts removed. Yet it would hardly have been less scruffy than in this picture, in blue at Kings Cross shed before the war. Photograph J.T. Rutherford, The Transport Treasury.

Of the many aspects of life which were dependent on the railway one area which has virtually disappeared is the transport of troops by train. John Aird, who lived near Closeburn in Nithsdale, Dumfries-shire, enlisted and proceeded to join the 70th training battalion of the Royal Scots at Berwick on Tweed on 15 January 1942 and kept a record of many of the journeys he made by train. Under the restrictions of military discipline it was not always possible to obtain details of locomotives and movements. In his words, beginning that day 15 January 1942:

LMS Compound 914 pulled into Closeburn Station on the G&SWR main line some twelve miles north of Dumfries on time at 9.22am having left Glasgow St Enoch station at 7.00 that morning for Carlisle. I had joined the army much to the annoyance of my father who thought I should stay at home and help him run the family farm. However, the chance of adventure was too strong, I was en route for No.10 Infantry Training Centre at Magdalene Fields Camp, Berwick-on-Tweed, close to Marshall Meadows signal box.

The camp was situated next to the East Coast main line and our squad hut was only 50 yards from the railway fence. Memories are of enormous loads and power combinations. For example I recollect the 10.00am Waverley to Kings Cross, still named 'Flying Scotsman', slowing down for the Berwick stop hauled by A4 Pacific 4490 EMPIRE OF INDIA with *nineteen* coaches. This sort of thing was fairly commonplace. The army ration of coal for our hut was fairly niggardly and we found it necessary to augment it. Although strictly against regulations it was the practice to 'liberate' lumps of coal from the trackside. Unfortunately one of our number was apprehended by the railway police and in addition to the coal in his possession he was charged with the 'larceny of a wooden fence rail, the property of the London and North Eastern Railway Co'. He eventually appeared before the magistrate at Berwick Petty Sessions and was fined 5 shillings with 11 shillings costs! Needless to say we all had a whip round to meet the bill.

In February I went home to Dumfries for weekend leave. This involved travelling with the 11.25am (Berwick to Kings Cross) behind A3 2565 MERRY HAMPTON, a K3 to Carlisle and a Class 5 up to Dumfries. Due to the poor connections on a Sunday on my return I had long waits at both Carlisle and Newcastle. The train from Dumfries was the 10.00am from Glasgow St Enoch to St Pancras hauled by Kingmoor Black 5 5152. I recollect that at Carlisle the loco for the forward journey to Leeds was 5X 5566 QUEENSLAND. Whilst in Carlisle I also saw 6222 QUEEN MARY on the late running 10.00am Glasgow Central to Euston. I travelled from Carlisle behind Raven Atlantic 698, reaching Newcastle around 9.00pm. The next train north was the 2.55am express to Edinburgh behind V2 4890, arriving at Berwick on a snowy morning just in time for reveille. My 170 mile journey had taken 20 hours!

In April, having completed our basic training, we moved to Dumfries by ordinary passenger train. We left Berwick at 8.08am for

WAR REPORT ... WAR REPOR

St Boswells via Reston Junction, a line that was to be closed after the 1952 floods. There we joined a Waverley to Carlisle train hauled by one of the elusive Canal A3s, 2567 SIR VISTO. This had three through LMS coaches for St Pancras and included an LNE restaurant car, despite their withdrawal from most main line services for the duration of the war.

After a few weeks we were on the move again and the company, equipment and baggage were loaded at the former Caledonian Railway goods station in Dumfries. The equipment was carried in horse boxes. We proceeded tender first behind 5X 5732 SANSPAREIL over the ex-Caledonian branch to Lockerbie and then to Slateford, Edinburgh. Getting out, I noticed 5X 5584 NORTH WEST FRONTIER passing through in charge of five corridor coaches on a southbound train. I also had my first sight of an ex-CR 4-6-2T. Several local journeys were made by train whilst at Redford barracks, one to an athletics event behind 2920, a V1 2-6-2 tank. The principal journey was to a ten day exercise based at the then tented

Pennyland Camp at Dumfries House near Cumnock in Ayrshire. The last stage of the journey was completed behind an LMS Crab 2-6-0. We detrained at Auchinleck and completed the journey on foot. The routing was via Glasgow and Kilmarnock despite the alternative and more direct cross country course via Carstairs and Muirkirk to Dumfries House station on the A&C line. Our return to Edinburgh was from Machline Station and whilst waiting there a double headed northbound express passed through behind Compound 1140 and 5X 5611 HONG KONG.

In August 1942 when based at Dunglass, East Lothian, I was granted one month's 'agricultural leave' to help my father with the harvest. Imagine my surprise, waiting at Cockburnspath station for the Berwick to Edinburgh Waverley local, when it arrived behind A4 4490 EMPIRE OF INDIA. I travelled to and from home via Glasgow as was usual.

In October 1942 my company was sent by road to the Duns area. The platoon was billeted at a former AA gunsite at Slighhouses about six

miles from Duns, Berwickshire. For a period of some three weeks we helped with the potato and sugar beet harvest. Conditions were wet and muddy to say the least. Army boots were woefully inadequate and we looked with envy at the farm workers who had long rubber waders! One of our jobs was to accompany a tractor and trailer to Reston station on the East Coast main line with sugar beet which was loaded into open wagons bound for the factory at Coupar (Fife). The nearest bus to civilisation was from Chirnside six miles away, where there was a service to Berwick. A trip to the pictures involved a twelve mile return walk to Duns. The 'townies' amongst my mates took very badly to this isolation.

We moved to Duddingston Longs early in November and two weeks later were on the move again, in a train of LNE tourist stock overnight from Duddingston to Upminster, Essex. The journey commenced behind Haymarket V2 4807. We were due to arrive at 4.27am but were thirty minutes late, hardly bad for wartime. Whilst unloading the train I saw my first Stanier three cylinder

Jubilee 5566 at Camden before it acquired its QUEENSLAND nameplates (in April 1936) with the Turbomotive behind. This engine took John Aird forward from Carlisle when returning from leave in 1942. Streamlined Pacific 6222 QUEEN MARY ran past on the late running 10.00am Glasgow Central to Euston. Photograph W. Hermiston, The Transport Treasury.

You'll Remember those Black and White Days...

2-6-4T 2502 on a Southend train. The platoon was billeted in a private house at 7 Hall Lane, near the station.

I went home for Christmas from Euston (10.10am to Perth). At Carlisle I joined a Stranraer train to Dumfries arriving after midnight and in the absence of any road transport had to walk the twelve miles home. The return journey from Dumfries was made behind 5X 5725 REPULSE and at Hellifield I saw the recently rebuilt 5735 COMET running light engine. On that trip I had to stand all the way to Leicester. The loco from Leeds to London was Patriot 5538 GIGGLESWICK. In February 1943 I was transferred to the 11th Battalion Royal Scots Fusiliers then based in Chepstow, Monmouthshire.

Our draft left Upminster in reserved accommodation behind a Tilbury 4-4-2T, 2160. We went into Fenchurch Street station and then transferred to the Underground (Circle Line) to Paddington. We left Paddington by the 11.55am South Wales express and arrived at Newport at 2.40pm where we changed and travelled by a semi-fast train to Chepstow. Whilst there,

during off duty times it was popular for the troops to visit the fleshpots of Newport and to return on the 11.45pm express from Newport to Paddington which was routed via Chepstow. Complaints were received from the GWR of frequent evasion of fares by the troops. Stern warnings were issued by HQ of disciplinary action against those detected!

In April, I was a member of an advance party sent by road to Pennylands Camp, Auchinleck, Ayrshire, where we had exercised the previous year. The journey took three days! The main body of the Battalion followed by train. Within a few weeks the entire 49th Infantry Division, of which the Battalion formed part, *returned* to South Wales and Monmouthshire by train. The battalion reoccupied its old accommodation at Bulwark camp, Chepstow. This, we later learned, was due to a change of plan which had originally earmarked us for action in the invasion of Sicily.

On return to Chepstow I was transferred to Divisional HQ at Whitney Court, Whitney-on-Wye which was located on the Hereford and Brecon branch of the LMS, itself

a relic of the Midlands Railway's forays into Wales. There were just three trains into Hereford, on weekdays only. These were 'all stations' and, we were convinced, the slowest in the country. From memory they were powered by ex-L&Y 0-6-0s in the 121XX series.

In June 1943 the 49th Division returned to Ayrshire and promptly reoccupied the accommodation that had left a few months before! I was still at divisional HQ and we travelled by special train from Whitney on Wye to Troon, Ayrshire. Divisional HQ was set up in two large houses on the southern outskirts of Troon near Lochgreen Junction. In September 1943 I was at Kilmarnock station returning home on leave when I saw the 9.15pm ex-St Enoch to St Pancras behind rebuilt Royal Scot 6103 ROYAL SCOTS FUSILIER. This was closely followed by the 09.27pm ex-St Enoch HM Forces only train which I joined. This ran by Dumfries and then the West Coast main line to Euston. It was hauled by Stanier Pacific 6236 CITY OF BRADFORD and had several sleeping cars, for officers only. This was the first occasion I saw colour light signals

V1 2-6-2 tank 2920 before the war, which took the author and mates to an athletics event while at Redford barracks. Photograph W. Hermiston, The Transport Treasury.

You'll Remember those Black and White Days...

WAR REPORT ... WAR REPOR

One of the elusive Canal A3s, 2567 SIR VISTO on the turntable at Haymarket. Photograph J.T. Rutherford, The Transport Treasury.

on the G&SWR main line – between New Cumnock and Kirkconnel. On return from leave I rejoined the battalion at Auchinleck.

In November 1943 we were taken from Auchinleck station to Ardrossan (Montgomerie Pier) station behind a Hughes Crab. This involved a reversal at Lugton East Junction and a run over the former Caledonian Railway Lanarkshire and Ayrshire extension. At Ardrossan (Montgomerie Pier) we embarked on SS *Hantonia*, a Southern Railway cross channel ferry, for the voyage to Inverary where I spent three weeks on assault training which included much jumping out of landing craft on the shores of Loch Fyne. The return journey was by the same route but this time we sailed to Ardrossan aboard the Isle of Man Steam Packet Co vessel *Ben-my-Chree*.

In early December a period of leave came round which I decided to spend with relatives near Liverpool. At Kilmarnock I caught the HM Forces overnight train from Glasgow to Euston hauled by 6229 DUCHESS OF HAMILTON, alighting at Dumfries, the last official stop, at around 11.30pm. At midnight, off the Stranraer line came Royal Scot 6169 BOY SCOUT piloted by a Fowler 2P 4-4-0. This is the only time I have

seen or heard of a 'Scot' on the 'Port Road'. Arrival at Carlisle was at 00.45am in time to see Black 5 5484 on the overnight train from Glasgow to Manchester and Royal Scot 6134 THE CHESHIRE REGIMENT on the Liverpool equivalent, on which I travelled. The train ran via Wigan and St Helens to Lime Street. Incidentally, Liverpool Exchange station had been closed for part of 1941 and most of 1942 after bomb damage to bridges outside the station. During this time long distance trains terminated at Liverpool Kirkdale. On arrival at Lime Street station the train engine by this time was 5X 5631 TANGANYIKA. I then travelled from James Street station on the Mersey Railway to Meols in the Wirral. The train consisted of the then new 1938 LMS stock but the elderly Mersey Railway coaches were used on trains to New Brighton. At the end of my leave on the return journey north the motive power was Black 5 5046 between Liverpool and Carlisle. I was taken forward from Carlisle to Dumfries by the 10.30am ex-Leeds to St Enoch behind Royal Scot 6108 SEAFORTH HIGHLANDER.

There was another trip by Mogul on 16 December 1943, from Auchinleck to Wemyss Bay for embarkation to Rothesay on the *Glen*

Sannox. The train ran via Kilmarnock, Barrhead and Muirhouse Junction. Whilst we were there we took part in further assault landing training at Blind Man's Bay at the south end of the Island of Bute. The trips there were made on board the *St Seriol* of the Liverpool and North Wales Steamship Company, which in peacetime sailed daily in summer from Liverpool to Llandudno and the Menai Straits.

In early January 1944 a visit was made to the 49th Divisional assault course at Sherrifmuir near Dunblane where a replica of the Atlantic Wall had been built for further battle training. Although this was around 70 miles from Pennyland we were taken by lorry.

The day for leaving Scotland came on 14 January 1944 when the battalion was marched round Auchinleck behind a military band and loaded onto a ten coach military special headed by Kingmoor Black 5 5363 bound for Great Yarmouth. Over the Settle and Carlisle we had an MR Class 3 4-4-0 as pilot. I awoke to find the train entering Melton Constable, the former HQ of the M&GNR and we arrived at Yarmouth Beach behind a GE 4-4-0. I was billeted at the Morton Private Hotel in Regent Road where, in the absence (as usual) of any furniture

WAR REPORT ... WAR REPORT

we slept on the floor. In late January 1944 I used leave to visit family friends at Upminster; travelling via Norwich, Ely and Cambridge behind B12 8580 we were seriously held up by an air raid. On the return I saw my first B1, 8306 BONGO, at Ipswich. Several other journeys were made by rail around this time to places in Suffolk for training purposes and to Colchester for rifle practice. In early April a trip was made from Yarmouth South Town to Brandon via Ipswich for a visit to the 'Stanford practical training area' on the Norfolk/Suffolk border. My last visit to London was by the 2.15pm express from Norwich (Thorpe) behind Sandringham 4-6-0 2839 NORWICH CITY. This was probably the fastest express from Norwich to London during wartime and a place on it was much sought after. On other occasions I had to make do going via Thetford, Ely and Cambridge, taking more than four hours.

On 22 May 1944 we were unexpectedly given 47 hours leave and I travelled from Yarmouth Beach to Peterborough stopping at all 37 stations. There I caught a train pulled by V2 4883. At Leeds I transferred from Central to City station to join the overnight train from St Pancras to St Enoch. On leaving Leeds this train was powered by 5X 5587 BARODA piloted by Black 5 5187. From Carlisle the pilot was

Compound 4-4-0 909. I managed to spend all of twelve hours at home and that night made my way back to Dumfries where, at 11.15pm I joined the London overnight express again behind BARODA, this time without a pilot. When I left the train at Leicester I noticed that the ten coach train was by now hauled by 5X 5604 CEYLON. I then met up with some of my colleagues and travelled via Stamford to Peterborough; here we changed once more and joined an M&GN all stations train from Peterborough (East) which departed at 10.33am. We did not arrive at Yarmouth until about 3.00pm, behind Holden 4-4-0 8829. I was promptly rebuked by the Company Sergeant Major for being one hour late!

There was an air of expectancy in early June about the forthcoming invasion particularly as our motor transport was sent to Tilbury. On the morning of 6 June I was kept awake all night by the sound of aircraft passing overhead and at 3.00am we were roused and marched to South Town station where a train was waiting. We heard about the Normandy landing around 5.00am over the regimental wireless sets as we passed through Ipswich. We went through the eastern suburbs of London and detrained at Snaresbrook and marched to a camp at Wanstead flats where troops intended to take part on the 'D Day'

landings had been quarantined. On the morning of 9 June we were taken to Waterloo and boarded a train for Southampton there to join the Bibby liner *Cheshire* for our cross channel journey.

On 25 June I was wounded and after a rather rough crossing back across the Channel arrived at Portsmouth. On 30 June I was evacuated by ambulance train from Portsmouth to Chertsey station and then to Botleys Park War Hospital. Only a few days later, on 2 July, I was taken on board an LNER ambulance train complete with Geordie crew and set off for Manchester (Victoria) via Leicester and Chinley. As I could not see out of a window I had to rely on a neighbour to relay information on progress on the journey. Needless to say the NE crew were most partisan, making caustic remarks about the pulling power of LMS engines and comparing them unfavourably with LNER Pacifics!

On 25 July I was deemed fit enough to travel home. The first stage of the journey from Manchester was behind Black 5 5222 from Victoria to Hellifield where I joined the 4.47pm express from London bound for Glasgow behind 5X 5639 RALEIGH without the help of a pilot. I was soon to be discharged from the Army and my rail journeyings at the King's expense were over!

One reason every journey took so long of course, was the disruption caused by enemy action – this scene at Brentwood, to the east of London, in 1940 was typical.

You'll Remember those Black and White Days...

Pride in the Job

Guard Ray Ruffell was a memorable figure, as these pictures certainly demonstrate. The rebuilt Merchant Navy at Waterloo was heading a Pirelli Special (obvious enough you might say) about 1963. Pirelli had factories in the Southampton area so this could be either the return of a staff outing to the capital, or a party special for a works visit down at Southampton. The train crew, immaculate guard and overalled enginemen, happily pose alongside. The other scene is Bournemouth West in 1964; this time Driver Ernie Harvey poses with Ray Ruffell alongside 34026 ROUGH TOR. Photographs A.J. Sumpter collection, Jamie Lester.

You'll Remember those Black and White Days...

Pannier Portrait
Observations by Leslie Tibble

Pannier tanks might seem familiar enough but close-ups like this always repay a good look. Our portrait is 5757 at an unknown location – though it could well be Maiden Newton; the station had a bay/loop platform on the Up side as I recall. If so, 5757 is standing in the Up platform, with the photographer on the Down. Pannier 5757 carries an 82D Westbury shedplate and is coupled to an auto-coach, though the 57XXs were not push/pull fitted. These front end views show clearly the GWR lamp brackets (they had to be different!) and spare lamp in position on the running plate. The closer study shows very clearly the elongated slot in the drawhook (drawbar) to house the screw coupling. It's summer with vacuum hose pipes coupled but not the steam heat pipe below the buffer beam. The 'bow end' of the auto coach is also clear. Typical GWR corrugated iron PARCELS OFFICE & CLOAKROOM beyond, with guard of old bullhead rail to prevent damage by luggage, trolleys and so on. Photographs The Transport Treasury.

You'll Remember those Black and White Days...

Three railwaymen, including typical Driver with bag, watch the photographer. Shown clearly is the operating mechanism for the gravity sanding – running in front of leading splasher and behind spare lamp and brackets and then running behind the middle driving wheel splasher en-route to the cab. Photograph The Transport Treasury.

Close detail of the injector. That's an oil feeder wedged behind it, the oil keeping warm for easy flow! Can anyone explain the 'dent' in the hand rail in front of the casing for the injector delivery pipe? Photograph The Transport Treasury.

You'll Remember those Black and White Days...

BR early emblem freshly cleaned, a common shed practice, together with a clear view of tool box and clasp. Coal slaking pipe hanging down and wrapped around footstep. That looks like a fire iron lying on top of pannier tank, the injector delivery pipe to the top feed preventing it falling off! Photograph The Transport Treasury.

Very clear view of steps and hand rails affording access to bunker. Sliding vent open on cab rear. That's the vacuum train pipe I would guess running along the side valance. What's puzzling is the padlock and chain on the fire iron bracket. The padlock should be securing the tool box but perhaps 5757 had a regular crew (or crews) who'd rather secure the fire irons to prevent them being 'acquired' by others? Photograph The Transport Treasury.

Merrie England

Beautiful Battersea, with W 2-6-4T 31924 of Hither Green heading towards Factory Junction and home in the early 1950s with a freight, from Old Oak Common or Willesden – the headcode was the same from either. The train is on the SE&CR's Ludgate Hill branch, having come down the West London Line. There were seven of these trips to/from Willesden and five to/from Old Oak Common on a normal weekday. Battersea Power Station is prominent as is Hampton & Sons' Depository which stood alongside Stewarts Lane shed yard – note also the coaling plant and water tank. The photographer is standing on the embankment of the LBSC South London Line from Battersea Park Junction to Factory Junction. The low level lines to the right of the loco, where the coaches are stabled, are the original LCD main lines. To the right of these, on the viaduct, is the replacement 1867 route – two up lines, the 'Up Metropolitan' and Up Main and just the one Down Main. Photograph Lens of Sutton Collection.

Ramsgate's 34078 222 SQUADRON crosses Margate Road viaduct on the last lap of its Victoria-Ramsgate journey in the 1950s. A somewhat prettier prospect than the one above but every bit as fascinating, perhaps. And both places, indubitably (the sign proves it) part of Merrie England... Photograph Lens of Sutton Collection.
Notes by Bryan Wilson.

You'll Remember those Black and White Days...

Fourum Highland Holiday, 1953

Trains were few and far between on the Highland Section in the early 1950s, distance and single track reinforcing the remoteness. Cars were hardly an answer; for a start few could afford them and the narrow roads winding for miles over the hills were often not much better than tracks. Apart from that it rained a lot. We know little of Roy Wilson's hols, except that he was at Kyle of Lochalsh (above) on 26 July 1953. The station and quay lay just round that bend where the 0-4-4T is shunting; the inevitable Perth Black Five waits in the yard of the little two road shed for its next turn to Inverness. The next day (below) finds us at Inverness and another Perth Black Five, 44979, bound for 'the North'. Photographs R. Wilson, The Transport Treasury.

Another day on, 28 July, and another Perth Black Five, 44975. The train is in the line to the right of 44979 (bottom left). Later that same day we are back at Kyle (below) and dear old 55216 is still shunting. It was a relative newcomer, transferring from Perth in August of the previous year. Photographs R. Wilson, The Transport Treasury.

You'll Remember those Black and White Days...

DIESEL DAWN Barely a Decade
Notes by Ronald H. Edge

The first of the class, D8400, cleaned up (possibly for the last occasion in its career) for the May 1961 exhibition of stock at Marylebone Goods Yard, held to celebrate the Golden Jubilee of the Institution of Locomotive Engineers. Brush Type 2 D5699 (new in April that year) at the front and the tender of MALLARD at the cab end.

In the May 2002 issue of *British Railways Illustrated* Ray Fox and Mike Kinder detailed the bewilderingly wide-ranging faults and shortcomings of the North British diesel prototype 10800: *It should perhaps be mentioned that despite the seemingly endless problems listed above, NBL actually built ten 800hp Bo-Bos in one of the ill-fated Pilot Schemes – D8400-D8409 in 1958. How far 10800 was regarded as a basis for these is unclear, though there was certainly a close resemblance, in appearance at least. The engine was different though, and the generator and traction motors were by GEC not BTH. There was one marked similarity – the D8400 locos were subject to constant problems and they too were withdrawn a mere ten years after they were built.*

There was of course no hint of problems to come when the D8400s were unveiled as 'Light-Service Diesel-Electric Locomotives for British Railways' in the railway press in the summer of 1958.

Five classes of diesel locomotives of 800-1000bhp (they were not yet known as 'Type 1s') were ordered in the initial stage of the British Railways modernisation programme at the end of 1955 and the D8400s made up the third class to be introduced. The Paxman engines

were the same as those in the earlier D8200 series. Like the EE D8000 series and the D8200s, the new locos were Bo-Bos with a single cab close to one end. 'As the envisaged duties are principally in connection with freight trains' the official specification read, no train-heating equipment was installed. The new units had dimensions as follows:

Axle arrangement: Bo-Bo
Top speed: 60 mph
Service weight: 68 tons
Wheel dia: 43in
Bogie wheelbase: 8ft 6in
Bogie pivot pitch: 20ft
Length over buffers: 42ft 6in
Starting tractive effort (28% adhesion): 42,000lb
Continuous rated tractive effort: 20,000lb
Fuel capacity: 490 gallons

The locos were of conventional construction. Underframes were in standard rolled sections but with cast-steel dragboxes at the ends. Bogies were swing-bolster with a dished centre pivot to transmit the superstructure weight, the pivoting action and the traction and braking forces.

The side frames were flanged plates, formed into box section. A laminated spring along the centre

line of each frame formed the primary suspension for the SKF roller-bearing axleboxes.

Oerlikon/Davies & Metcalfe straight air brakes were provided, with vacuum equipment for the train brakes. There were two 8in cylinders mounted on each bogie to operate the clasp clocks on each wheel, with the cylinders carried transversely on the headstocks. The Oerlikon three-cylinder two-stage compressor, driven by a Crompton Parkinson motor, was located in the forward end of the engine compartment; for the vacuum brake there were two Reavell exhausters and these, with their GEC driving motors, were housed in the short compartment behind the cab.

The Paxman 16YHXL engine and main generator was carried on a four-point resilient mounting beneath the welded steel combined sump and common underbed. The engine was the modern four-valve-head direct-injection model of the by then well-known 7in by 7¾in cylinder engine, which dated back to 1938. Over the years it had been upgraded in the successive RPL, RPH and YH classes to take advantage of experience, new materials and techniques and so on. The normal traction rating was 1,000bhp at 1,250rpm but to suit the

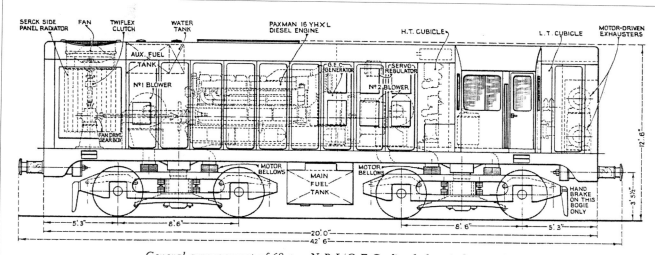

General arrangement of 68-ton N.B.L. G.E.C. diesel-electric locomotive

power requirements of the D8400s the power setting was arranged at 800bhp and 1,250rpm.

The new locomotives came into service as detailed below. Some form of trial/test must have been conducted, though there does not seem to be any readily available record of it. The unlamented 10800 had undergone test working on the LTS lines for a few days in 1955 and if the staff at Stratford recognised or knew of the antecedents of D8400 then it would have certainly been greeted with something approaching circumspection...

D8400 to Stratford May 1958
D8401 to Stratford June 1958
D8402 to Stratford July 1958
D8403 to Stratford July 1958
D8404 to Stratford August 1958
D8405 to Stratford September 1958
D8406 to Stratford September 1958
D8407 to Stratford September 1958
D8408 to Stratford September 1958
D8409 to Stratford September 1958

The D8400s were intended for use on freight services more or less local to London, including inter-Regional workings to Hither Green and New Cross Gate. As well as this they were to be used on parcels trains from Liverpool Street out onto the Southend line. They seem to have remained almost invisible so far as the railway press was concerned, unsurprisingly given all the momentous events through the rest of the 1950s and the 1960s. Fortunately some indication of their

The new loco ('for light-service duties in the Eastern Region') in official pose, 1958.

You'll Remember those Black and White Days...

service history is available from the records of the Motive Power Committee. Early indications, in May 1959, were good:

week ending	oper. total	% avail. 24 hours
18/7/59	10	90%
25/7/59	10	90%
1/8/59	10	90%
8/8/59	10	80%

These figures seem reasonable enough and indeed the official comment expresses every confidence: 'These locomotives continue to perform in a most satisfactory manner.' A month later the Motive Power Committee concluded: 'These locomotives continue to be most satisfactory.' At this time the similar-looking BTH Type 1s in the D8200 series (ten were based at Devons Road on the LMR) were held to be giving 'generally good service' while the twenty EE D8000 Type 1s (of the five classes of Type 1s eventually built these were the only ones to survive the 'great cull' of the late 1960s) 'presented no difficulty in service or maintenance during the period under review'.

By May 1961 the D8400s were suffering somewhat:

week ending	oper. total	% avail. 24 hours
29/4/61	10	50%
6/5/61	10	60%
13/5/61	9	67%
20/5/61	10	40%

Inside the cab; controls were duplicated for movement in either direction. Diagonal NBL plate on bulkhead reads North British Locomotive Co. Ltd. and The General Electric Company Ltd., with the year, 1958, in the centre.

Engine repairs and collision damage had affected availability, while their increasing use on shunting further limited the mileage. By the latter part of 1961 availability dipped at times to 40% as two locomotives underwent intermediate repairs for most of August and part of September. Fuel pump problems reduced availability and mileages further as the year wore on. By the end of 1962, however, availability was 90% and mileage was up, with all ten working 'satisfactorily'.

So the D8400s seem to have avoided the disasters that accompanied the introduction of 10800 back in 1950, at least in the first few years. The locomotives nonetheless led an undistinguished

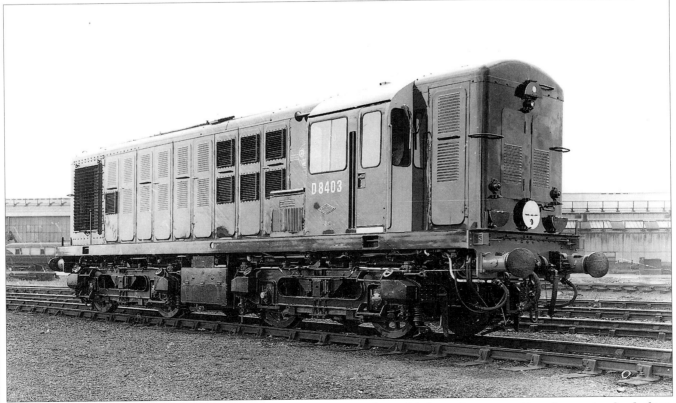

D8403, new on arrival at Stratford in July 1958. The irony is that withdrawal, as a small and non-standard class, would have been decreed in 1967 anyway – even if they had been completely perfect in service.

life through the 1960s. There were engine problems that reduced availability, spares and so on became more expensive and difficult to obtain and the sort of trip freight and shunting work to which the D8400s were suited steadily evaporated. In 1967 BR announced a programme to reduce its varied diesel fleet, disposing of all those classes that were small, non-standard or particularly troublesome in service. It was a dismal outcome, involving as it did whole classes of a hundred or more. In all this the disposal of the D8400s was, naturally enough, barely noticed: D8404 went in February 1968 and all the rest had followed by the September, representing barely a decade in service for each of the locomotives. All had been scrapped before the end of the following year.

Above and below. **D8400 at what looks like Temple Mills, in May 1959. NBL worksplate proper on cabside.**

You'll Remember those Black and White Days...

The lads observe D8403 at Temple Mills with a transfer freight bound for Hither Green, 8 July 1961. Photograph F.W. Goudie, The Transport Treasury.

D8402 (the curious interpretation of the two-tone green livery was a pleasing feature of all the smaller Type 1s – the D8400s and D8200s as well as the Claytons and the WR D9500s) on typical work at Stratford Low Level, 26 August 1961. This was precisely the sort of work which was soon to disappear. Photograph Frank Hornby.

A3s On Shed

Super sights of A3s, at Gateshead shed on 3 July 1955. The actual site (it was a vast and sprawling place) is the collection of three short sidings at the west end, on built-up ground above the so-called 'rabbit banks'. The main shed is behind the photographer, the Tyne some distance below, over to the right, and the running lines parallel to the great river are over on the left. At first glance the look of the three engines seem to confirm all the worst of Gateshead's reputation for lax cleaning, yet only the V2 60957 is a Tyneside native. 60081 SHOTOVER comes from Neville Hill and 60098 SPION KOP from Haymarket. Photograph Eric Webb, The Transport Treasury.

60081 SHOTOVER again, this time in a rather better state of cleaning, at home at Neville Hill shed, Leeds, some months earlier on 4 September 1954. It's not quite clear what the Fireman is doing but the photograph demonstrates once again that handrails on steam locomotives were quite often footrails too... Photograph Eric Webb, The Transport Treasury.

You'll Remember those Black and White Days...

Fourum Summer Saturday at The Warren

It's Saturday 28 August 1954 and the stage is set for a procession to be savoured. So settle back in the sand, finish off that Walls' ice cream between its two wafers and await the next train... First, Castle 4-6-0 5095 BARBURY CASTLE rounds the curve at Dawlish Warren with the fourteen coach 11.00am Paddington to Penzance. A few minutes later (below) comes 70021 MORNING STAR, one of the new Britannias that was so perturbing Laira at this time, with the closely following 11.05am Paddington-Penzance. Photographs R.C. Riley, The Transport Treasury.

You'll Remember those Black and White Days...

It's now the turn of Castle 5071 SPITFIRE to distract the sunbathers, while working the 11.25am Cardiff-Penzance. Observe the subtle social currents; 1950s couples in coats, hats and ties contrast with a bikini clad bathing belle – as *Picture Post* doubtless would have put it (top left – notice the bloke close by is preparing to watch the *train*, not the lady...). Below, an unidentified Castle heads the 8.06am Sheffield to Kingswear. In the distance in all these pleasant views lies the East Devon coast, with Exmouth out of the picture to the right. Photographs R.C. Riley, The Transport Treasury. *Notes by Eric Youldon, with the able assistance of Peter Gray.*

You'll Remember those Black and White Days...

Severnside Steam in the Middle Sixties
Notes and Photographs by Peter Kerslake

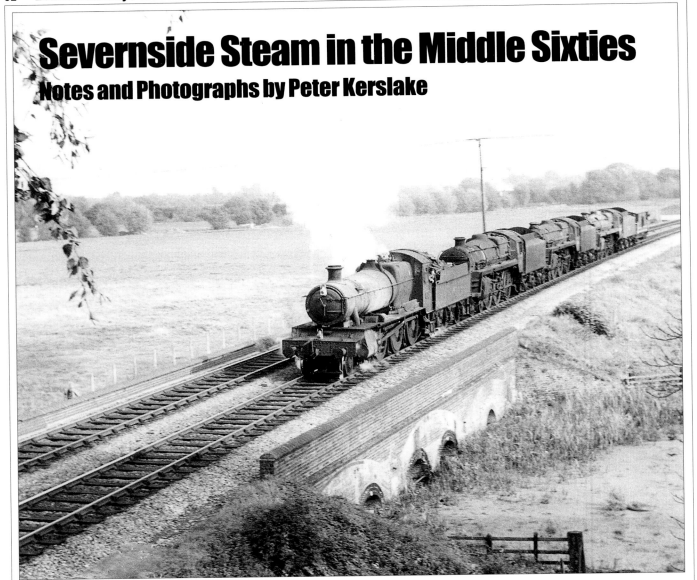

Despite the rapid decline of steam in many parts of the country by the mid-1960s it was still possible to find plenty of scheduled steam passenger and freight workings in the Gloucester area, well into 1965. An area of both London Midland and Western Region workings, Gloucester enjoyed a wide variety of steam locomotives and even following the cessation of steam workings on main line passenger services in September 1965 the high volume of freight, particularly to and from South Wales, ensured a continuing number of steam workings. It was a sad fact, however, that many fine locomotives from both Regions were in very poor external and mechanical condition, with many from the WR losing cabside numberplates and nameplates. Yet they were still worthy of being captured on film, particularly as their remaining days in service were, by the end of 1965, very limited indeed. There were exceptions, though, and occasionally a well groomed LMR 9F would appear at Gloucester Central Station heading a South Wales steel train. Sadly, amidst the run-down Halls and others, such uplifting sights were rare indeed. With the demise of the last few Castles the 1965 Saturday summer specials from the Midlands to the West Country were, in the latter part of that year's summer services, entrusted to LM Britannias. The Pacifics, despite their neglected outward appearance, always seemed to be working well as they ran through Gloucester. The final scheduled main line summer passenger working, on Saturday 4 September 1965 was, however, entrusted to 7029 CLUN CASTLE, which was specially selected to head that train from Bristol northwards to Birmingham, passing through Gloucester in fine style some fifteen minutes early just before 7pm. This was the last steam hauled scheduled passenger train between Bristol and the Midlands. I have attempted to portray here just a few of the more interesting scenes from Gloucester at that time.

Above. At 1.45pm on Wednesday 13 October 1965 7816 FRILSHAM MANOR, minus its nameplates, has the sad task of hauling a trio of condemned BR Class 5s to South Wales and the scrapyards. The sad procession is approaching Over Bridge, just west of Gloucester on the South Wales main line, and the Class 5s are 73015, 73051 and 73054. The latter was in excellent external condition and resplendent in green livery. My notes indicate that the three Standards had come from Bath Green Park shed on the S&D. 7816 had been a St Blazey engine in happier days and survived this particular run to Wales as she was back at Gloucester the following day. Photograph Peter Kerslake.

Bottom right. It was possible to see a Western Region engine in fine condition in 1965; on 14 July 6859 YIEWSLEY GRANGE is in immaculate green livery, after working a Royal Train (so I understand) in Wales a week or so earlier. The location is Gloucester Central station, and the engine was working up from South Wales on a freight. Alongside is 7816 FRILSHAM MANOR, also with a freight. Photograph Peter Kerslake.

You'll Remember those Black and White Days...

Above. 7915 MERE HALL makes heavy weather of restarting a north-bound freight from the South Wales line at Gloucester Tramway Junction (Horton Road shed is behind) on 4 January 1965. The engine had lost its nameplates two days earlier. Photograph Peter Kerslake.

You'll Remember those Black and White Days...

Western Region 2-8-0 3864 restarts after a brief pause at Gloucester Central, en route for the scrapyards at Risca in South Wales with three condemned locomotives on their final journey. The date is 21 June 1965 and in tow were 5955 GARTH HALL, LM 0-6-0 44135 and 4992 CROSBY HALL. All were from Barrow Road shed, Bristol and appeared to have been in open storage for a considerable period of time. Photograph Peter Kerslake.

A study in steam at Gloucester Horton Road shed, 9F 2-10-0 92138 receiving attention from the fitters on 4 January 1965. A brazier provides some crude comfort at least. Photograph Peter Kerslake.

Mainstay of the South Wales freights during the final months of steam on Severnside at this time were the Standard 9Fs – 92087 is heading through Gloucester Central from Wales with a train of iron ore bound for the north on 16 July 1965. Severn Tunnel Junction shed was still open to steam at this date but by October steam freight workings on the South Wales line had been substantially reduced, and by the end of that year had ceased. Photograph Peter Kerslake.

During the final months of steam around Gloucester it was possible on some Sundays to witness LMR locomotives, all in steam and coupled together, returning light to their home sheds. During the previous week they would have worked 'unbalanced' freights to Bristol and South Wales; a number of returning light engines would be coupled together on arrival at Gloucester whereupon they would head home in fine style, and usually at high speed. This is Elmbridge Bank, between Gloucester and Cheltenham, on Sunday 14 November 1965 and in the final weeks of steam one of the last such cavalcades goes by, 92215 heading 48752 and an immaculate 48417 with an unidentified 9F bringing up the rear. Photograph Peter Kerslake.

You'll Remember those Black and White Days...

TURKISH DELIGHT
Impressions of Turkish Railways, 1968
By Englishman Abroad, BRILL Kondüktör D.W. Winkworth

Westbound train consisting of DB stock, headed by 2-10-0 56511, about to leave Hadimköy on 3 September 1968.

A visit to Turkey to explore that country's railway system and find some British connection was made in 1968 and at the conclusion of the trip the findings were written-up for reference purposes. Thirty-five years on the notes have surfaced and, with the dust blown off, have jogged the memory.

No attempt has been made to up-date the writing; certainly things have changed in that the Tünel line in Istanbul has been rejuvenated and now has modern stock and the last remnant of the TCDD narrow gauge, Samsun to Carsamba, has been converted to standard gauge to mention but two differences. What follows tells it as it was way back in 1968, when despair at the end of UK steam drove many observers abroad. All photographs D.W. Winkworth.

Turkish railways have seldom attracted much attention in British circles. True, there is the Orient Express, the railway to Baghdad and the strong German affiliation; these apart, however, the image of TCDD (Turkiye Cumhuriyeti Devlet Demiryollari Isletmesi) is not particularly sharp, due to a variety of reasons.

Single-track trunk routes and a low speed restriction have not permitted any notable fast running with prestige trains whilst the late development of the system from a conglomeration of individual railways has been a continuing but unspectacular operation. For motive power the country has, until recently, always looked to Europe and designs have tended understandably to reflect the standard practice of the country from which the locomotives have originated.

Distance has done nothing to remedy this lack of attention although this drawback will perhaps be discounted now that, in an era of disappearing steam traction, the steam locomotive is assured of a place in Turkey into the 1970s. Be that as it may, a recent visit has shown that, with the consolidation of the system complete, modernisation has now begun to make its mark. Admittedly there is not much evidence of this as one rouses from a night in the Wagon-Lits vehicle of the Marmara Express to look out in the early morning on an arid landscape that is typical of Turkey-in-Europe. At the front of the train, if the distinctive tender is any guide, is one of the ubiquitous German - type Kriegslokomotiv 2-10-0s whilst towards the back is a restaurant car which is almost a period piece internally with leather-upholstered armchairs reminding one of the London club atmosphere.

Progress over the single line steel-sleepered track is steady. There is an occasional halt at a passing place to take water or allow another train to cross. At Cerkezhöy a 2-8-0, No.45506, awaits on a freight; later the morning diesel railcar from Istanbul, packed to the doors, passes and at Hadinköy there is an all-German ensemble with TCDD No.56511 (another Kriegslokomotiv) heading twenty or more DB six-wheelers forming what is possibly a seasonal workers' train. Just how far this rake is going is not clear but if the coaches are bound for their homeland, even if it is only Bavaria, then it will prove to be an arduous journey for the passengers.

No more traffic is met with until Halkali is reached. This is the outer terminus of the electrified suburban area of Istanbul and because of this the locomotive depot is relatively busy. In addition to further examples of the 45500 series of 2-8-0s there is No.46001 (a 4-8-0 of German origin) and some 44500 0-8-0s. At the back of the shed stands a disused relic in the shape of an outside framed 4-4-0.

The high running numbers of the locomotive stock is explained by the method TCDD uses in incorporating the wheel arrangement into the numbers. The first figure denotes the number of coupled driving axles,

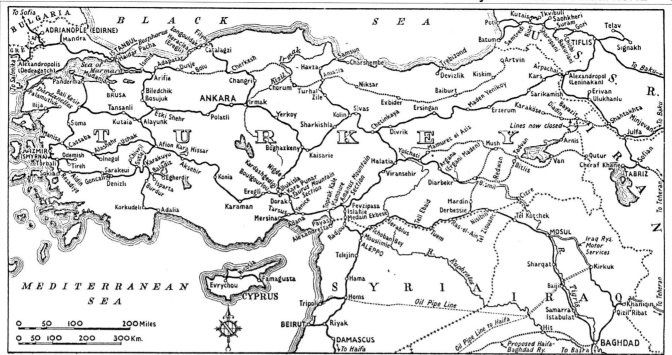

There are slight variations in spelling between map and text – those in the text were current in 1968. Dotted lines indicate proposals rather than construction.

the second the total number of axles and the remaining digits are the running number of the locomotive within the axle grouping. Tender locomotives always have a total of five figures but tank stock (with the exception of narrow-gauge examples) have four. Because eight-coupled engines are very common in Turkey the English enthusiast with strong London Midland steam leanings will find such numbers as 45156, 45506 and 46224 striking a nostalgic chord.

Turkey registered a notable first in the Istanbul-Halkali electrification for, in addition to being the first electrically-operated section of TCDD it was the first regularly-operated suburban railway in the world to use 25,000v single phase 50-cycle ac with overhead wire. The opening day was December 4 1955. Multiple-unit sets painted brown with cream above the waistline operate the service, supplemented by three Bo-Bo locomotives constructed by Alsthom to power the locomotive-hauled trains. One of these machines takes over from the 2-10-0 and after a long wait follows a suburban train into Istanbul. Naturally this prevents

Halkapinar on 8 September 1968 with 2-8-0 45131 on a Ciyli-Izmir (Basmane) service. Note star and crescent on sides of rolling stock. The well-known railway photographer, author and traveller P. Ransome-Wallis was patrolling Europe in an earlier decade and along with description and insight his writings are peppered with the sort of comment we are less likely to see in modern times. This is a gem: *In the cities, broken-down cars, taxis and lorries are parked in the streets, and on the morning after my arrival in Istanbul it required five taxis to take me from my hotel to the Sirceki station; each one broke down or its tyres were punctured. Each time the jehu hailed another cab and refused to take any fare or tip. It took an awful long time to get to the Sirkeci station but it was the cheapest taxi ride I have ever made. The delays need not have worried me as the 'Balkans Express' which I had come to see, was two hours late.*

A 4-6-4T, 3706, about to leave Haydarpasa with the 9.20 train to Tuzla on 5 September 1968. Reconstruction works for electrification are in progress.

any speed being attained, the colour light signals being constantly passed at the caution aspect. The eighteen miles of the electrified line are double-tracked and the stations have island high-level platforms. The route is along the shore of the Sea of Marmara and at one point cuts through the city walls; shortly before the terminus of Sirkeci is reached the branch to the train ferry (this links the European and Asian parts of the TCDD system) is thrown off. This trans-continental traffic is confined to freight.

Sirkeci station is the headquarters of traffic division No.7 (Turkey-in-Europe) and is peculiar in having low platforms for main line trains and normal British height for the suburban traffic. Customs examination takes place here for the international traffic. Across the station, on the suburban side, under cover are two preserved items of rolling stock on display, the eye-catcher being 0-4-0T No.2251 built by Krauss in 1874 (builder's number 380). The nearby explanatory notice states it was used on the Istanbul-Edirne route until 1954, was withdrawn in 1964 and restored together with its companion exhibit in 1967. The companion is a four-wheel carriage which belonged to Sultan Abdulaziz and was used, a year after its construction by Cammell, for the inauguration of the Edirne route in 1873.

The older part of Istanbul surrounds the Sirkeci station; linking this to the newer part is the Galata Bridge (this marks the lower end of the Golden Horn incidentally). In the newer part is to be found, a few steps from the bridge, the only other form of railed transport in the city, the independently-operated underground funicular known as Tünel. Opened in January 17 1875 it employs the unusual gauge of 1510mm (4ft 11in) and has two tracks throughout its 650 metre length (nearly all in tunnel). On each of these is a two-car train – constructed by MAN – worked by cable on the counterbalance principle. The track has welded joints but the hand of modernisation has yet to touch the four-wheel cars, as clerestory roofs and varnished timber panelled interiors and exteriors bear testimony.

Each car has three sliding doors and longitudinal seating (seats but not the backs are upholstered) in eight bays giving a seating capacity of 32 persons each vehicle. The route is dead straight although

TABLE 1
PRINCIPAL EXPRESS PASSENGER TRAINS IN TURKEY-IN-ASIA

Name	Between	Number of services operative each week in each direction	Distance Miles	Journey Time Hours Outward/Inward
ANADOUI EXPRESS	Istanbul (H) Ankara	7	359	11¾/11½
DOGU EXPRESS	Istanbul (H) Erzurum	7	1067	41¼/39¾
	Istanbul (H) Kars	5	1208	47/46
GUNEY EXPRESS	Istanbul (H) Kurtalan	3	1146	44¼/45¾
IZMIR EXPRESS	Izmir (B) Ankara	3	519	15¼/14¾
TOROS EXPRESS	Istanbul (H) Baghdad	2	1595	71¾/70
VANGOLU EXPRESS	Istanbul (H) Tatvan	2	1175	52/53¼
RAILCAR TRAINS				
BOGAZICI MOTOTREN	Istanbul (H) Ankara	7	359	9¼/8¾
CUKUROVA MOTOTREN	Ankara Adana	2	418	12½/12¾
EGE MOTOTREN	Izmir (B) Ankara	6	519	13¼/13½
MARMARA MOTOTREN	Bandirma Izmir (B)	3	214	7/7¼

the gradient – averaging 1 in 10 – is not constant throughout the 200 foot rise. It is steep at the upper end and less pronounced, indeed almost level, at the foot. Electric operation is conducted from controls at the top terminus. Each terminus has turnstiles to admit passengers and tickets are not issued on entry to the platforms. There is invariably a lot of traffic offering in both directions and the trains are seldom without standing passengers. Outside the upper station is a trolleybus terminal point which undoubtedly adds to the traffic for the railway, to become a link in the commuter chain from Galata Bridge to the Pera district and to the suburbs beyond. Proposals have been made from time to time for an extension of the railway under the Golden Horn to the Stamboul district but these appear to be as far from fruition as ever.

Cooks Continental Timetable advises that four hours should be allowed for transfer from Sirkeci station in Istanbul to the Asian terminus of TCDD at Haydarpasa across the Bosporus (but twice as long in the reverse direction!) although one suspects this wisely allows a recovery margin for late running of trains because the ferry journey occupies no more than twenty minutes. The ferryboats leave the landing stage adjacent to the Galata Bridge and are very skilfully navigated in the congested waters of the harbour. Haydarpasa pier is dominated by the great mass

of the station and office building. Inside there is a spacious concourse leading to the platforms, which have recently been rebuilt in connection with the forthcoming electrification. It is the intention to electrify initially the main line from Haydarpasa to Ankara, then on to Irmak and finally to Zonguldak, on the Black Sea coast, a total distance of no less than 660 miles.

Haydarpasa is the headquarters of traffic division No.1 which extends as far as Eskisehir; other divisions are Ankara (2), Izmir (3), Sivas (4), Malatya (5), Adana (6) and, as already noted, Sirkeci (7). Its traffic on the main trunk route is worked principally by diesel-electric locomotives. After a small pilot order for Co-Co type machines was delivered, a larger one was duly executed by General Electric (of America) in the 1964-65 period for the firm's U20C model of that wheel arrangement in the 2,150/2,000 hp range. Painted red with broad cream lines and lettering they see service throughout the country on the more important of passenger trains. Pending electrification the suburban traffic between Haydarpasa and Gebze continues to be worked by 3700 class 4-6-4 tanks, built by Henschel in 1925 and assisted by the 1932 vintage 46000 4-8-0 locomotives built by the same firm and also by Krupp.

By autumn 1968 overhead wire was in position in a few places in the suburban areas, standards had been erected in profusion and a new

stock shed was virtually complete at the terminus but a lot of work remained to be completed including alterations to the alignment and track layout at various locations. The suggestion that 1969 would see the overhead wire energised and two tracks in use as far as Arifiye seems extremely unlikely to be fulfilled.

Locomotive-hauled trains (other than suburban or local services) usually provide three classes of accommodation; first class seats two a side, second class three and third class four a side. Additionally some trains such as the Taurus Express offer Pullman and Wagon-Lits standards of comfort. All accommodation is usually in heavy demand. Diesel railcar trains are usually first and second or second class only and equally well patronised.

On the Haydarpasa-Ankara line the best scenic stretches are along the coast of the sea of Marmara in the region of Kartal and on the climb out of Bilecik. Apart from the Adapazari branch at Arifiye there is little steam traction to be seen between Izmit and Bilecik but at the latter place a couple of the German-built 5700 class 2-10-2 tanks, specially constructed for assisting on the eastbound climb, are usually in attendance. Bilecik also seems to mark the limit of steam traction operation from the Eskisehir direction. This route is probably as typical as any in Turkey in the day-to-day minutiae which strike a visitor as unusual. These include

0-8-0T 4401 at Bilecik on 5 September 1968; water and food vendors await the next train. Ransome-Wallis again: *The Turks are charming, helpful and hospitable people but the masses are not highly intelligent, nor are they disposed to do more work than is absolutely necessary...*

You'll Remember those Black and White Days...

Light shunting duty for Stanier 2-8-0 with a Black Five number, 45154, at Samsun docks on 15 September 1968.

the habit of travellers taking their seats over an hour before a train starts, the inadequate number of first class seats in the train (seldom more than sixteen places) and members of permanent way gangs using prayer mats at the appropriate times of the day. There are vendors of hot skewered meat (kebab) and bread and various other edibles – and in some cases items of apparel – parading their delicacies and wares up and down the train; hordes of children besiege the trains at stations selling anything from water at three pence a bottle to melons and bags of grapes and peaches; then there is the travelling train cleaner who clears rubbish out of compartments and nonchalantly tosses it out of the window. Eskisehir is a divisional boundary point and also has a locomotive repair works which is still active – it rose to building a locomotive not many years ago – as well as being the junction for the routes to Izmir (previously known as Smyrna) and Konia. The quickest way to make the journey from Istanbul to Izmir is by boat to Bandirma and thence by rail via Balikesir; consequently the traffic for Izmir passing Eskisehir

No.46246, an American built 2-8-2, at Alayunt with 6.40 Eskisehir-Balikesir service on 6 September 1968. Notice the ladder on the water column to attend to the lamp – it was by no means a standard feature.

2-10-0 No.56523 entering Balikesir at head of the 13.24 ex-Bandirma on 6 September 1968.

comes from Ankara rather than Istanbul. There are, in each direction, a diesel-hauled night express, a day diesel rail car service plus a local train between Eskisehir and Balikesir which appears to be the preserve of one of Balikesir depot's allocation of 46200 class of USA-built 2-8-2s. The southward route from Eskisehir dates back to 1896 when the railway was opened as far as Konia. At Alayunt there is a triangular junction with the 1932 line to Balikesir, which has become the principal route to the Aegean coast from the east. A good quantity of freight traffic is handled over this route, almost exclusively by 44000 class 0-8-0 locomotives.

The southern exit from Balikesir is heavy graded and the heavier trains require piloting assistance. These pilots, from Balikesir depot, work as far as Soma and will be, more often than not, one of the Ministry of Supply USA-built type 2-8-2s originally used in Persia, Syria and the Middle East. It seems a little incongruous at first to find locomotive types constructed by opposing sides in World War II working trains in tandem, for the train engine will probably be a German 56500 class 2-10-0; on reflection it will be realised that Turkey has acquired a good range of steam locomotives built for that conflict. In addition to the two types mentioned there are also the Stanier 2-8-0s from British builders and the US Army Transportation Corps 'S160' 2-8-0s.

At Manisa the old route from the east to Izmir is joined. The French company, the Smyrna-Cassaba and Extensions Railway, reached Cassaba in 1866 and eventually extended as far east as Afyon. After that it enlarged its mileage by building northwards to Soma (opened in May 1890) and finally established a line right through to Bandirma on the Sea of Marmara coast. The Afyon-Manisa section is now comparatively little used with but one passenger train over the length of the line every 24 hours.

From Manisa the railway remains single-tracked, even in the Izmir suburban area as it sweeps round the Bay of Izmir, until Halkapinar where the short branch from Bornova joins it at the three-platform station. Immediately south of the station is the principal locomotive depot of Izmir. A high fence prevents any sight being obtained of activities round the shed and, in any case, the diesel traction building completely blocks a view of the steam section. At Hilal there is a crossing on the level of the route from Izmir (Alsancak) to the south and a few moments later the passenger from the north will be in the spacious terminus of Basmane. The platforms are completely unprotected from the weather although the circulation concourse beyond the buffer stops does have a barn-like erection to protect travellers from the elements.

Izmir is possibly as interesting a railway centre as any in Western Turkey for the enthusiast. Movements from both termini may be kept under observation very easily at Hilal crossing. Suburban services operate frequently from Basmane to the Bornova branch and along the main line to Ciyli and Menemen and from Alsancak to the Buca and Seydiköy branches. Some of these trains load to 19 or 20 four-wheelers. Local trains beyond the suburban area operate to such destinations as Alasehir, Tire and Odemis. To these are added the long distance services. Motive power for these trains ranges from the 0-8-0s of the 44000 series, Humboldt-built 2-8-0s of 1912 vintage and 57000 series lightweight 2-10-2s to Robert Stephenson 2-8-2 products of 1929. This last type was a small class of which at least two (Nos.46103 and 46104) remain in use. Another Stephenson engine – 0-6-2T No.3412 – keeps them company if only on shunting duties at Basmane, but the same manufacturer's 0-8-0s and 0-8-2 tanks may well have gone to the scrap yard by now. Main line diesel locomotives are in a minority on Izmir trains at present. Railcars form a few local as well as one or two long distance services.

In contrast to its neighbour at Basmane the terminus at Alsancak offers good cool cover for its patrons and seems to reflect the English idea of a train shed – this was the headquarters of the English-owned Ottoman Railway which started operation as long ago as Christmas Eve 1860. The nearby locomotive

Izmir (Alsancak) station with 0-8-0 44062 on 12.15 departure to Seydikoy and 44031 light engine, 7 September 1968.

shed has diminished in importance, now acting as a stabling point for diesel shunters which work in the nearby dock area.

Alsancak remains the principal departure point for the southward route to Denizli although there are one or two diesel railcar services which use the connecting curve at Hilal and Basmane terminus. South of Izmir there is initially a climb followed by less arduous terrain through Torbali, junction for the Odemis branch, as far as Selcuk, the station nearest the ruins of Ephesus.

After Selcuk there is a very long and severe climb during the passage of which the ruins of the ancient city may be discerned, albeit at a distance. By Ortaklar the climbing

No.44062, an 0-8-0, approaching Hilal crossing with Buca-Izmir (Alsancak) train on 7 September 1968. The rolling stock is kept commendably clean in Turkey.

British product, 0-6-2T 3412 at Izmir (Basmane) would not be out of place in a Welsh valley. 7 September 1968.

is over and the route is through flat country as far as Goncali, the junction for Denizli. The Humboldt 2-8-0s operate the branches all round the southern loop, with 56500 2-10-0s and 57000 2-10-2s on the main line traffic. The exception is at Nazilli, a curiosity in the shape of a four-wheel Ruston-built tractor and a few four-wheel coaches operating a service from a platform divorced from the main station.

This service does not appear in the timetable; this, however, is not particularly remarkable because TCDD's timetable does not include every service operated. Two editions are issued, an abridged version of main line services and a more

detailed book which nonetheless fails to include local services for Ankara, Istanbul and Izmir. In late 1968 the most recent issue of these tables was dated May 1966 and the abridged version only was then available. This reflects the static nature of the services in general.

The southern loop turns northwards at Goncali and joins the Konya route at Afyon where reversal is necessary to continue to Eskisehir. Moving across from the western part of the country to Ankara the pattern is little different. The western approach to the new capital is across a plain; the suburban area is marked by the commencement of double track (at Sincan) much of it concrete sleepered upon which the USA 2-8-2s perform briskly running tender first in the westward direction due to lack of turntables or turning layouts. Ankara's station is not a terminus which reflects the comparatively recent accession of this city to the position of capital. At the time railways were first proposed in Turkey, Smyrna and Istanbul (or Constantinople as the capital was then known) were the most important towns and it was natural that these places should be focal points for the new mode of transport. Consequently Ankara (Angora as it then was)

became a town served on the route from Constantinople to Sivas and its eventual elevation in status came too late to affect the railway map.

The eastern exit from Ankara is heavily graded and explains why the 2-8-2s on the suburban trains work tender first on the westward run. Double track extends as far as Cebeci although the suburban traffic goes a little further to Kayas. Whereas the main line traffic between Haydarpasa and Ankara is the monopoly of the diesel-electric locomotives this is rather less marked beyond Ankara. At Irmak, the junction for the 300-mile long route through important industrial areas to Zonguldak, examples of the American built 2-10-0s of the 56300 class are to be found. These engines have a distinctive fairing each side of and atop the boiler, hiding domes and chimney, and are readily recognisable.

After Irmak the next railway centre is Kayseri (nearly 600-miles from Istanbul) which is the operational but not the physical junction for the route to the south through the Taurus mountains to Adana and along the southern boundary of the country to Baghdad. Kayseri is a locomotive changing point as well as a divisional boundary and during the wait in the station it is not unusual to find officials going through the train checking the quantity of cushions in each compartment against the inventory of the coach, a ritual not entirely appreciated when the train is

TABLE 2
PRINCIPAL STEAM LOCOMOTIVE CLASSES

Nos	Wheels	Builders	Date
44001-10	0-8-0	Linke-Hoffman	1924
45001-62	2-8-0	Tubize	1929
		Nohab	1934
45501-18	2-8-0	Batignolles	1925
46001-25	4-8-0	Henschel	1933/5
		Krupp	1932
46051-62	2-8-2	Henschel	1937
46101-6	2-8-2	Stephenson	1929/32
46201-53	2-8-2	Baldwin	1942
		Lima	1942
56001-168	2-10-0	Henschel	1937
		Vulcan (UK)	1948
		Skoda	1949
		TCDD	1961
56301-88	2-10-0	Vulcan (USA)	1948
56501-53	2-10-0	Acquired from German sources	
56701-48	2-10-0	Acquired from SNCF 1955	
57001-27	2-10-2	Henschel	1935
		Krupp	1932
3701-8	4-6-4T	Henschel	1925
5701-4	2-10-2T	Henschel	1952

Stephenson 2-8-2 46104 (works number 3996 of 1929) heading the 12.15 Izmir (Basmane) to Menemen local train at the (railway) level crossing at Hilal. Note signal cabin on the left. 8 September 1968.

running several hours late! Eastwards the route makes its way to Sivas, where there is a locomotive works which shares with the one at Eskisehir the distinction of building a locomotive to a design already in operation. Sivas is the operational junction for the line serving Samsun over 240-miles by rail to the north on the Black Sea coast. Here the remaining length of TCDD narrow gauge is met with, running eastwards to Carsamba and worked by 2-6-0Ts. The Samsun line has Nohab 2-8-0s of the 45000 series working the passenger trains and Stanier 2-8-0s acting as dock shunters at the port itself. At Cetinkaya there is a further junction on the eastern route. The main route proceeds to Erzurum and eventually Kars (about 1,200 miles from Istanbul); it was on this section the TCDD had, until about 1961 when it was converted, a length of 75cm gauge line between Horasan and Sarikamis. Beyond this there was the 5ft 0in gauge section connecting Sarikamis with Kars. The southern route from Cetinkaya goes to join that from Adana to Baghdad, throwing off at Malatia another route which bifurcates at Yolcati to serve Kurtalan and Tatvan and, by means of boat, Van.

A system running through trains for lengths varying between 500 and 1,000 miles (see Table 1) over single track is perhaps not to be taken to task for a certain amount of late running especially as time, to the Turk, is not considered to be the

most valuable of life's gifts. Punctuality is a very variable factor. West of Ankara during a period of ten days of observation the late running was seldom very bad for, apart from the Marmara Express, nothing worse than a 30-minute deficit was noted. East of the capital matters were rather different with some trains hours late and not readily identifiable so far were they out of course. The worst example encountered was an arrival at Sivas six hours late which, instead of allowing a connection to be made and an arrival at Samsun to be effected at 19.54 one day, caused the fulfilment of that intention to be delayed until 11.20 the following day. Another 2¼ hours on the advertised arrival of that particular train gave an effective late arrival of 15½ hours. In mitigation it may be recorded that during the foregoing ordeal the writer was given a couchette *gratis* and a beverage attendant provided breakfast – on both counts 'for the tourist'.

Steam locomotives (see Table 2) are painted black with red wheels, although at least one tank engine has been seen in green livery; the diesel-hydraulic shunters are painted red; motor trains are decked out in red and white or cream and ordinary passenger stock is dark green. Freight stock (most of which is 'fitted' or 'piped') is finished red and grey and lettered TCDD. The crescent and star is featured on all stock other than freight and is etched on carriage windows.

Signalling is either colour light or of German semaphore type but is not universal for there is none at all on the southern loop through Goncali. Centralised Traffic Control is planned to go hand-in-hand with the new electrification works. Stations are usually masonry structures although in the south-west area there are some timber erections notably at Denizli which is a very poor example for a town of its size. Modern buildings have been erected at Afyon and Eskisehir and elsewhere.

As well as the electrification works an extension is under construction from Tatvan eastwards to Iran. Steam traction will be progressively superseded, the diesel-electric machines displaced from the newly-electrified lines taking over their duties. Already shunting turns are passing from steam to diesel-hydraulic power and the older types of small steam shunter have disappeared. There is very little container traffic at present and not much interchange of freight stock with other countries. The maximum speed limit for steam passenger trains is 50mph, for railcars 78mph and freight trains 37mph. Will the Turkish modernisation plans mature too slowly is the principal query in Western mind for, already, giant articulated lorries can be seen passing through the towns of Asia Minor operating a Hamburg-Munich-Teheran service...

2-8-0 45027 leaving Samsun on the Black Sea with the 9.05 train to Sivas, 15 September 1968.

More confusing numbers 2-6-0 34013 working in the docks area of Samsun on 14 September 1968.

Endpiece

Last checks. Photograph Barry Richardson, The Transport Treasury.

You'll Remember those Black and White Days...